In this delightful tour of the Old [Testament,] [Chad Bird] [brings] out the beauty of God's gracious [gospel] [in each and every sto]tory that culminates in Jesus Christ. He shows how the major events and characters of the Old Testament reveal humanity's desperate need for, and God's wondrous provision of, redemption of sinners based on divine mercy alone. What a joy to read and what a blessing to the church!

Dane Ortlund
Author, *Gentle and Lowly: The Heart of Christ*
for Sinners and Sufferers

In this journey through some of the major episodes of the Old Testament narrative, Chad Bird is the most reliable and fascinating of guides. With every step, Bird illuminates both the extraordinary and the mundane aspects of the narratives with a keen eye for their Christological significance. *Hitchhiking with Prophets* is such a pleasure to read! By the end, the reader will not only have a grasp on key people and events, but a sure faith in the God whose certain promises outstrip the sin of his all-too human people.

Todd Brewer
Managing Editor, Mockingbird Ministries

It is easy to find yourself lost within the pages of the Old Testament. The history, culture, language, geography, politics, and laws are all a bewildering challenge for the modern reader. What one needs is a map to help you navigate the terrain. *Hitchhiking with Prophets: A Ride through the Salvation Story of the Old Testament* is such a map. In this book Chad Bird will guide you through the Old Testament as he points out the key people and theological ideas in God's unfolding redemptive plan. Chad's understanding of the storyline of Scripture makes this a map worth keeping close as you travel through the pages of the Bible. *Hitchhiking with Prophets* is an excellent guide for the new or even the not-so-new explorer of the Old Testament.

Dr. Chris Hulshof
Associate Professor of Bible and Theology
Rawlings School of Divinity
Liberty University

This book is something better than a hitchhiker's guide to the universe. It's a grace-filled, salt-seasoned celebration of the first part of the best book in the world. Here you'll find the meaning of life, the universe, and everything—if you let Chad Bird pick you up and drive you home to Jesus.

James M. Hamilton Jr.
Professor of Biblical Theology
The Southern Baptist Theological Seminary

People travel all the time to see amazing sights. Reading a book can be like taking a trip. You should open *Hitchhiking with Prophets* and take a ride through the salvation story of the Old Testament. With accessible and lively prose, Chad Bird guides you through the wonders and tragedies and highs and sorrows of what's going on in the Old Testament. Along the way, and most importantly, we see the covenant faithfulness and mercy of the one true God who has made the world and is committed to redeeming it through a Promised Son.

Mitch Chase
Associate Professor of Biblical Studies
The Southern Baptist Theological Seminary

Hitchhiking with Prophets is the work of Chad Bird at its best. First, it emphasizes the Christ-centered nature of the Old Testament. Bird repeatedly highlights how every prophecy, mediator, and institution of Israel points ahead to Christ and new covenant. Secondly, the work shows how grace is the central moving force of the biblical narrative. In a word, Bird demonstrates how from age to age the people of God are sustained by Word and sacrament, in spite of being nothing more than a wrecked little flock of sinners.

Jack Kilcrease
Associate Professor of Historical and Systematic Theology
Christ School of Theology
Institute of Lutheran Theology

HITCHHIKING with PROPHETS

A RIDE THROUGH THE SALVATION STORY OF THE OLD TESTAMENT

CHAD BIRD

HITCHHIKING with PROPHETS

A RIDE THROUGH THE SALVATION STORY OF THE OLD TESTAMENT

Published by:
1517 Publishing
PO Box 54032
Irvine, CA 92619-4032

Publisher's Cataloging-In-Publication Data
(Prepared by The Donohue Group, Inc.)

Names: Bird, Chad, author.
Title: Hitchhiking with prophets : a ride through the salvation story of the Old Testament / Chad Bird.
Description: Irvine, CA : 1517 Publishing, [2024]
Identifiers: ISBN: 978-1-956658-85-9 (hardcover) | 978-1-956658-86-6 (paperback) | 978-1-956658-73-6 (ebook) | 978-1-956658-87-3 (audiobook)
Subjects: LCSH: Bible. Old Testament—Introductions. | Salvation—Biblical teaching. | BISAC: RELIGION / Biblical Commentary / General. | RELIGION / Biblical Commentary / Old Testament / General. | RELIGION / Christian Theology / General.
Classification: LCC: BS1140.3 .B57 2024 | DDC: 221.61—dc23

Printed in the United States of America.

Cover art by Zachariah James Stuef.

Table of Contents

Introduction

I had no idea where I was. My legs, decorated with mud splashes and thorn lacerations, told the tale of my unwelcome adventure. An hour before, I had laced up my running shoes and hit the dirt paths in a nearby park for a long Saturday morning run. I was a newbie to this area and certainly a novice explorer of this sprawling park, which was veined through and through with a network of interlocking trails.

At first, everything was fine as wine. A cool morning. A mixture of sun and shade danced on the surface of the trails. But somewhere along the way, I turned left down a narrow, circuitous path and became disoriented. Without a phone or GPS to tell me where I was, I ran this way, backtracked, ran that way, backtracked, and wound up as lost as lost can be. Finally, spotting rooftops, I abandoned the trails to muscle my way through thorns and thistles until I stepped onto the welcome relief of asphalt.

As I stood there, hand shielding my face from the sun, looking left and right down unfamiliar streets, a car pulled up beside me. The window rolled down and I squatted to look across the cab into the gentle, smiling face of an elderly woman.

"You look lost," she said.

"Yes ma'am," I laughed, "afraid I am."

"Where do you live?"

"On Stoney Bend, off Wetmore Road."

"Oh, I know where that is. It's on the other side of the park."

"I guess so. I got all turned around on the trails."

"Well, get in. I'll give you a ride home. You look all tuckered out."

"Are you sure? I can probably find my way back."

"Yes, I'm sure. You'd probably just get lost again. Hop in."

And so I did. Along the way, my driver gave me the short version of her life, her growing-up years in San Antonio, her fifty-five-year marriage, and what a rough time she'd had getting used to the loneliness of widowhood. I mainly just listened. She seemed glad to have somebody to talk to. A few minutes later, as we pulled up in front of my house, I thanked her profusely for her generosity, then watched her drive away with a smile on her wrinkled face.

It was a short ride and a short conversation, but my unplanned hitchhiking experience turned a stranger into a temporary acquaintance, opened up her life to mine for a few minutes, gave me a lift that I needed, and made her day because she was able to share her story with an active listener.

Sometimes, when you're lost, catching a ride with an old storytelling driver is the best way to get home.

This life of ours has no shortage of stories about us getting lost and trying to find our way home. Disorientation seems to be our direction of choice. When I was a young man, one of my teenage friends took his own life. For a time, I waded through a swamp

of grief, not knowing how to find my way home. As
a pastor, there were times I was so turned around by
disappointment, stress, and fear that I thought down
was up and up was down. Much later in my life, as a
truck driver on the night shift, I got lost dozens of times
in the network of ruts that sliced through the rough
Texas backcountry. At that time, I was also lost spiritually in a blinding storm of shame and self-loathing
from destructive mistakes of my past. While I was in
the middle of writing this book, my twenty-one-year-
old son, Luke, died in a hiking accident in Chile while
he was studying abroad as a midshipman in the United
States Naval Academy. Three and a half months later,
my eighty-one-year-old father died of a massive heart
attack. To say that I was "lost in grief" is a gross understatement. Eyes blind from weeping, I stumbled my way
forward through the fog of pain and frustration and
agony of soul I had never come close to feeling before.

Those are my stories of being lost. And I am willing to wager that you have no shortage of your own.

I suppose, when we're honest with ourselves, that
it's no real shock when we're lost; what seems a miracle
is when we finally get back home.

Getting back home is what this book is all about.
By "home," I don't mean your street address, your
mom and dad's house, or whatever place you think of
as safe. Home is where our Father created us to dwell.
And where our Father created us to dwell is in his Son,
Jesus. He is our home, where we abide, where we are at
peace, where we can finally look around and say, "Ah,
now this is where God wants me to be."

To get back home, to get to Jesus, is both a long
way and a short way. It's a short way because Jesus is

not kicking it back in some faraway celestial resort, light years from Earth, staring at stars while serenaded by seraphim. He's as near as your skin, as near as red is to the blood in your veins. As his apostle wrote, "He is actually not far from each of us, for 'in him we live and move and have our being'" (Acts 17:28). He's that close.

But, at the same time, to get to Jesus is a long way. By "a long way," I mean that Christmas didn't happen on the heels of creation. Noah didn't log onto Amazon to purchase Christmas gifts for his three sons, nor did Abraham, David, Nehemiah, or any of the other folks we will talk about in this book. First there was creation, then the cosmos got jacked up by our first I-know-better-than-God parents. Then came a whole long and tattered line of murders, plagues, exiles, kings, and prostitutes, along with lots and lots of thumb-twiddling. We're not talking years or centuries but millennia—thousands of years crawled by while the Lord's people were waiting for that "long way" to come to its divinely ordained finale.

That "long way" is what this book will document, in as vivacious and colorful a way as possible. For the Bible is not some dusty and boring textbook. It's a veritable circus of humanity, with clownish buffoons, high-soaring saints, back-talking donkeys, left-handed kingslayers, bewitching maidens, child-killing kings, naked preachers, and all the glory and gore you can fit inside the big top of this biblical tent. And everywhere in this story is God who, in his wild and passionate love for humanity, is shepherding history toward the birth and ministry of Jesus the Messiah.

Do you already have a good grasp of the Old Testament? Wonderful. This book will be an enjoyable review. Do you not know the difference between the Bible and *The Hobbit*? Also fine. This book will be a helpful map into unknown territory. By the time we're done, you won't know all the ins and outs of the story, but you will have a strong grasp of the major movers and shakers.

Our goal? To get home to Jesus. And to get there, we're going to hitch rides with some gray-haired storytellers. Abraham will drive us from Haran to the promised land, down into Egypt and back again, and all the way onto a lonely mountaintop where God had told him to do the unthinkable. We'll stick out our thumbs to the octogenarian Moses, who will pick us up near a fiery bush, steer us between ten plagues, race on dry soil between two walls of water, and finally drop us off in the Judean wilderness. With David, we'll drive through the pentapolis of the Philistines and take on monstrous Goliath. With Isaiah, we'll make some pit stops at prophetic oases. And with many other sages and preachers, we will sit shotgun and listen to them drop pearls of Hebrew wisdom into our open ears.

Each storyteller will take us a little farther down the Old Testament road. Each one will build on the stories of his predecessors. And each one, with a twinkle in his eye, will tell us to be on the lookout for the promised Seed. For at the end of the road, he is the one they—and we—have all been waiting on.

So, get in and buckle up. Let's ride.

Resources:

If you are looking for a podcast that gives you a brief but broad survey of the Bible's entire story—Old Testament and New Testament—check out "A Field Guide to the Bible," a podcast in the 1517 Podcast Network. In twenty-seven episodes, totaling only about eleven hours of listening time, I join my friends Daniel Emery Price and Erick Sorensen to guide you through the major events and individuals of the Bible, from Genesis to Revelation.

What about a deeper and longer dive into the Old Testament? A verse-by-verse, chapter-by-chapter discussion of every book, from Genesis onward? We've got you covered in the podcast "40 Minutes in the Old Testament." My cohost, Daniel Emery Price, and I began with Genesis 1 back in 2015, and we are still moving forward today. So, if you want to dig into the nitty-gritty of the story and wrestle with all the details and events, then join the vast network of other listeners.

For a vast array of other resources on the Bible (free classes, daily articles, videos, books, conferences, and more), visit 1517.org.

Chapter 1

Humanity's Mom and Dad

Warning: we're starting our journey a bit awkwardly. In the front seat are humanity's mom and dad—and they're both in their birthday suits. Strange, I know, but that's how our story begins. So, climb into the back seat, avert your eyes, and just listen. We've got a vast territory to cover in a short amount of time, all the way from a garden paradise to the east of Eden, past a cemetery full of graves. And along the way, a bright light of hope begins to shine. Welcome to where it all began: Genesis 1-5.

At the beginning of the Bible's story, we meet a Father who never tires of handing out gifts to us, his children. He's giving us a wide world that he built and a specific garden that he planted. He's giving the Pacific Ocean, ponderosa pines, the Milky Way, and hummingbirds. He is God the Giver to humanity the receiver. As he does so, he's dotting his I's and crossing his T's, double-checking every tiny particle of creation, to make sure we have the perfect home to dwell with him. Because dwelling with him is what it's all about. He is our Emmanuel, a Hebrew name that means "God with us." And if God is with us, and we are with him, then that, my friends, is paradise come true.

The opening chapter of Genesis is a day-by-day documentation of how the Lord is a builder, but a highly unusual one. He did not pull up early on a Saturday morning at the celestial Home Depot to purchase a truckload of earth, air, fire, and water to piece together a world. All he did was open his mouth. "Let there be light," he said, and light there was. "Let there be an expanse," he said, and an expanse there was. Words alone were his tools. He spoke everything into existence. And this is not a one-off thing with him. It's God's ongoing mode of operation. He speaks, stuff happens.

We learn something vital from this: the origin of everything not-God was, and still is, the word of the Father. Or, to be more precise, *the Word* of the Father. For, as the story rolls on, we will see that his capital "W" Word is not a mere vocable; the Word is the Son of the Father. One of Christ's first followers, John, will tell us about this Son by hearkening back to Genesis: "In the beginning was the Word, and the Word was with God, and the Word [Jesus] was God" (John 1:1). Therefore, in the beginning was the Father, with his Son and Holy Spirit, creating the heavens and the earth.

We describe our world as a planet, but for the people of the Old Testament, it was envisioned as a big temple. God makes it, organizes it, and furnishes it for his habitation. Temples are carefully structured spaces, where everything and everyone has a place and function. That's what is happening in Genesis as the Lord creates, divides, forms, and fashions water, dry land, heavenly lights, plants and trees, and finally animals and humans. The Lord is meticulous about everything, but in a healthy way. He's not slapping something together, higgledy-piggledy. He's precise. He's exact. And he's pleased with his work, for seven times he applauds it as "good" and "very good." After six days of putting together this world, crafting his cosmic temple, the Lord rests on the seventh day. In other words, he moves in. Home sweet home.

Every temple has its priests, who offer sacrifices, pray, work, and serve as guardians of the holy things of God. Our world was—and still is—no different. The first two priests were a man and a woman whom the Lord made on Friday, day six of creation. They were like the rest of the world, in that the Lord brought them into being, but they were also unlike the rest of the world. We humans are part heaven and part earth, you might say. We bridge the gap between God and everything else.

How so? Adam was made from the soil and Eve from his side, but of them the Lord said, "Let us make man in our image, after our likeness. And let them have dominion over the fish of the sea and over the birds of the heavens and over the livestock and over all the earth and over every creeping thing that creeps on the earth" (Gen. 1:26). Nothing else in all creation was made in God's image and likeness, creatures who mirror the Creator, his walking and talking icons in this world. We are not biological products of evolution, souls trapped in a "bag of flesh," or one more cog in the machine of a cosmos where we are ultimately no more important than a snail or microorganism. Humans are priestly kings and queens who simultaneously serve the Lord in this worldly temple and have dominion over all other creatures.

After this panoramic view of creation, we step into a unique place in this world named Eden. This is a mountaintop area, the peak of which is a garden paradise. Animals frolic about. Fruit trees decorate the soil. And the waters of a river ripple outward and downward, dividing into four streams that bathe the rest of the world with the vitality of Eden. Here the Lord places his male priest called Adam and his female priest called Eve. If the world is a temple, then this garden is the Most Holy Place in this temple, for here the Lord walks about with his children. All is well. God dwells with the father and mother of humanity. Even while strolling about naked as a jaybird, they feel no shame, for they are utterly innocent. The world is as it should be. They are as they should be.

Adam and Eve have two main jobs. In Hebrew, these duties are to *avad* and *shamar* (Gen. 2:15). The verb *avad* is a multifaceted word. It means to work, serve, and worship. They will *work* the ground as farmers. *Serve* the Lord as his priests. *Worship* him as their God. The verb *shamar* means to watch, guard, and keep. Later in the biblical story, when the Lord has Israel make a tabernacle, and still later the temple, the priests *shamar* these sanctuaries to make sure nothing unclean enters the sacred space. Adam and Eve are thus the guardians of this mountain paradise.

In freedom, this husband and wife can work, play, worship, make love, raise families, and expand the borders of Eden as the human family grows. To sustain their ongoing life, they can eat the fruit from one special tree called "the tree of life." From another tree, called "the tree of the knowledge of good and evil," they are never to eat. It's the only "No" that God gives them. As their

Creator, he alone determines what is good and bad for them. There is no ethical system of rights and wrongs. And there certainly is no humanly devised morality by which Adam and Eve decide what is best for themselves. What is best for them is to live in the love, freedom, and joy of the Father. That is how they continue to flourish as human beings.

This flourishing, however, soon gave way to floundering and falling. We don't know how soon things fell apart. Hours? Days? Weeks? Whenever it happened, the train wreck of humanity was immediate, catastrophic, and ongoing. A serpent, whom the Bible later tells us was a rebel angel named Satan, tempted Eve. He lured her to question whether what God had said to her was true. What's more, he depicted the Lord as miserly, a divine Scrooge who was holding out on them, keeping them back from the humans they could be.

In response to this twofold temptation—to ditch God's word and to doubt his lavish love—Eve sank her teeth into the forbidden fruit. Adam soon followed suit, and before that food was digested, the entire creation died a death that is still an ongoing demise today. We inhabit a dying world.

The aftermath of this first human rebellion against our Creator was the shattering of peace and perfection. Humpty Dumpty fell off the wall of Eden, and we all know how that story ends. In the coming chapters, we will occasionally note how the Lord did a hard reset of creation, but each time the cracks in the soul of humanity began to show immediately. Only at the end of the story will there be a true and lasting new beginning in Christ.

With a lost Eden in our rearview mirror, driving forward into human history, we can confidently say that everything from tsunamis to suicides, from divorces to overdoses, from droughts to birth pangs, has the DNA of Genesis 3 all over it. Adam and Eve were booted out of paradise to fight stubborn soil and to eke out a life in a land that now seemed to be thumbing its nose at them.

Making matters worse, there was no snail-paced descent into the darkened chaos of evil, for the very next chapter of human history has yellow crime scene tape wrapped all around it. In Genesis 4, Cain, the firstborn of Eve, murdered his younger brother, Abel. Man murders man. The soil, once a blessed gift to humanity, was stained with the lifeblood of a man.

That fratricide is followed, in Genesis 5, with a genealogy, the sad refrain of which is "and he died… and he died…and he died." Graves soon pockmarked the face of a once pristine and lovely world. The Lord of life, contrary to what he wanted, introduced death to humanity. Long after, the apostle Paul summed it up this way: "The wages of sin is death" (Rom. 6:23). And those wages never go unpaid.

Smack dab in the middle of this gloomy account of How Everything Got Totally Jacked Up, a dazzling beam of light did begin to shine. In fact, this light served as a tiny, unsetting sun of hope from generation to generation. Before the Lord exiled our parents from Eden, he spoke these words to the serpent:

> I will put enmity between you and the woman,
> and between your offspring and her offspring;
> he shall bruise your head,
> and you shall bruise his heel (Gen. 3:15).

This curse upon the serpent was a blessing upon us. War had been declared. There would be enmity—hostile, deadly, ongoing battle—between those of God and those of the devil. But a day would come when the serpent would sink his fangs into the heel of a man who would simultaneously squash the head of that viper. Long after Eden, on a hill right outside Jerusalem, the Son of God and the offspring of Mary, Jesus, would die a cruel death upon the cross. But under his heel was the flattened, lifeless head of humanity's ancient foe.

The Lord would, in his own sweet and perfect time, set things right. That hope, like a vein of gold, can be traced all through the rest of the Old Testament story. And to the next chapter in that story, we now turn to hear about a floating Eden-Ark and its famous captain, Noah.

Chapter 2

A Floating Eden, Captain Noah, and the Tower of Confusion

The first few miles in our journey began with a green and beautiful paradise, but that eye-popping vista soon gave way to a dull, brown un-paradise where serpents lie, blood-soaked soil cries, and grave upon grave marks mortality. But before things get better, they get worse—much worse. Soon, we will need our vehicle to float, for corpses will sink into the black depths of a world-wide flood and a single ship will signal hope. And even after the waters dry up, humanity, never seeming to learn its lesson, will attempt to create an Eden divorced from God. Buckle up, for we are entering the outlaw land of Genesis 6-11.

Imagine a world where water makes you thirsty, the sun shines darkness, and we swim in fire. In this nightmarish world, forward is backward, and backward is forward. Everything is out of place, out of order, devolving into a monstrosity where "what should be" gives way to "what should not." Such is the world we meet, in all its ugliness, as we hitchhike our way into the pages of Genesis 6.

What began as Adam and Eve breaking bad by ditching the word of God and doubting his love, then quickly slouched into Cain staining his hands with his brother's blood, got even worse as humanity began to spread abroad on the face of the land. The first scene we come upon, not surprisingly, has sex written all over it. I say "not surprisingly" because if love makes the world go round, then very often sex makes the world go wrong. Between a man and woman, joined in marriage, sex is a gift of God, designed for pleasure, procreation, and the ongoing physical and emotional connection of the spouses. And for that very reason, this gift has always been—and, of course, still is—twisted by dark forces into a tool whereby to besmirch people's souls by actions and relationships utterly contrary to the nature created in them by the Lord.

What happened in Genesis? Details are very sketchy, so teachers of the Bible wisely steer clear of saying they have The Definitive Interpretation of events. Here's the account in brief: "When man began to multiply on the face of the land and daughters were born to them, the sons of God saw that the daughters of man were attractive. And they took as their wives any they chose" (Gen. 6:1-2). The pressing question is whether "sons of God" refers to believing men or celestial beings. Basically, one of two things went down: (1) either rebellious angels visited our world, lusted after women, and impregnated them, thus producing a hybrid race, or (2) men of faith married unbelieving women and had children with them. Either way, a type of sexual union not countenanced by God engendered disunity in the human race. Coitus created chaos. Backward became forwards. And things got real ugly, real fast.

How ugly, you ask? Well, check out these chilling words:

> The LORD saw that the wickedness of man was great in the earth, and that every intention of the thoughts of his heart was only evil continually. And the LORD regretted that he had made man on the earth, and it grieved him to his heart. So the LORD said, "I will blot out man whom I have created from the face of the land, man and animals and creeping things and birds of the heavens, for I am sorry that I have made them" (Gen. 6:5-7).

You'd be hard-pressed to find a more damning and depressing speech uttered in all world history. Barely are we six chapters into the Bible when the Creator is ready to toss the cosmos into the garbage, pour a bucket of gasoline over it, and grab a pack of matches. It's that bad.

Before we lose all hope, however, listen to this verse that immediately follows those words quoted above: "But Noah found grace in the eyes of the LORD" (Gen. 6:8 KJV). Grace. Favor. In Hebrew, the word is *chen*. Like a similar Hebrew word *chesed* (love, lovingkindness, steadfast love), the noun *chen* welcomes us into the warm and capacious heart of the Father, who never stops wanting what is best for his children. He always loves, always welcomes us home, always and everywhere desires for us to be with him and him with us. Our Father will do whatever it takes to ensure that all hope is never lost, that there is always a way of redemption.

Just as our salvation is found only in the one man, Jesus, so at this early stage in human history, on this one man, Noah, hung the hope of the world. He was not *the* Savior, of course, but he was a kind of foreshadowing of who Jesus would be and what he would do. And this is not uncommon in the Old Testament. Long before Christ was born, the Lord highlighted certain individuals who were types or figures of Christ (e.g., Adam, Melchizedek, Moses, Joshua, David, and many others). I like to think of them as a "trailer" of the full "Jesus Movie" to come. They whet our spiritual appetites by giving us a brief and incomplete glimpse of the full cinematic story that will fill the Gospel screens of Matthew, Mark, Luke, and John.

What kind of man was Noah? He "was a righteous man, blameless in his generation. Noah walked with God" (Gen. 6:9). He was also married, as were his three sons, Shem, Ham, and Japheth. Peter adds that Noah was "a preacher of righteousness," so presumably he also tried to convince others to repent, believe, and come to God (2 Peter 2:5 NASB). But his hearers were having none of it. The earth, we are told, was "corrupt in God's sight, and…was filled with violence…for all flesh had corrupted their way on the earth" (Gen. 6:11). This corruption, this hardening of the heart that says "No" to God and "Yes" to evil, is still why people live their lives in the darkness of unbelief, violence, and egotism.

The Lord revealed his plan to Noah. He said, "I have determined to make an end of all flesh, for the earth is filled with violence through them. Behold, I will destroy them with the earth. Make yourself an ark of gopher wood" (Gen. 6:13-14). In further instructions, the Lord details the size of this ship, the need for rooms and decks and food storage within it, as well as the plan to make it a floating zoo. Male and female pairs of animals—along with seven of a few kinds of animals—would join Noah and his family in the world's first cargo ship.

When everything was ready, when the people and animals were all aboard, the ark served as Eden upon the waters. The Creator began rewinding creation to Genesis 1:2, when the world was one huge body of water, with no dry land. He was doing that hard reset that I mentioned in the last chapter. He was undoing the world, not merely to destroy, but that he might redo it. There would be a new "Adam and Eve" (in this case four men and four women), along with the animals dwelling with them, as it had been in the garden in Genesis 2. As the rains kept falling and the ark began floating, all else began dying. "Everything on the dry land in whose nostrils was the breath of life died" (Gen. 7:22). Creation was purged. The world of humanity, who did not want life with God, got what they wanted instead: death apart from him.

And Noah? God "remembered" him, that is, he remembered him in a *memory-in-motion* sort of way (Gen. 8:1). He dried up the waters. Mountains and land appeared once more. And a dove, holding an olive leaf in its beak, signaled hope. A little later, the Lord made a covenant with Noah, even hanging his bow in the clouds—a rainbow—as a sign that never again would he shoot the arrows of a flood at the earth. After floating for a little over one year, the ark had come to rest upon the mountains of Ararat (8:4). As Eden was on a mountain, with Adam and Eve and the animals, so Noah and his family, surrounded by animals, disembarked upon a mountain to start creation afresh.

But just how "fresh" was creation? Perhaps an analogy is in order. Much later in the Bible, Peter will liken the flood story to the baptism story of every Christian. As those eight people were "brought safely through water," even so "baptism, which corresponds to this, now saves you" (1 Peter 3:20-21). Were Noah and his family perfectly saved from death by floating in the ark? Yes. Are Christians perfectly saved from everlasting death by the water of baptism? Yes. Are Christians, having been baptized, also still sinners who stumble, fall, repent, and are forgiven? Yes. Even so, after Noah and his family experienced this "flood baptism," their human natures were still weak and self-willed, sinful, and prone to evil. This hard reset of creation did not remove the malware in humanity, so to speak. Creation was fresh to an extent, yes, but also still rotting on the inside. In fact, after the flood, the Lord himself said that "the intention of man's heart is evil from his youth" (Gen. 8:21). The flood, necessary as it was, had not altered humanity's fundamental problem: our wayward, rebellious hearts that always lean away from the Lord and toward the false and worthless pseudo-gods of this world.

As evidence of this human propensity to evil, two stories fall on the heels of the flood account: one involving drunk, naked Noah, the other the construction of a vain worship tower.

Sometime after the flood, Noah got into farming—vineyard farming, to be exact. When grapes appeared and he made himself some wine, he also partook, with evident gusto, of this fruit of the vine.

The result? He "became drunk and lay uncovered in his tent" (Gen. 9:21). Sober, righteous Noah becomes drunk, naked Noah. His youngest son, Ham, walked in on his dad in this rather unflattering position, then sauntered outside to gab about it to his brothers. These older two brothers, to hide the shame of their father, walked backward into Noah's tent, blanket in hand, and covered him up.

When Noah awoke and sobered up, he uttered his only recorded words in the Bible: he cursed Canaan (Ham's son), then pronounced a blessing on the older two sons, Shem and Japheth (Gen. 9:25-27). Why he cursed the grandson (Canaan) and not the son (Ham) is a question that scholars still wrangle over, but the effect was the same: thenceforth, Canaan (the father of the later Canaanites, whom we will hear much about later) was to be a servant to his brothers and their respective family lines. While there is much in this brief story that we do not understand, what is clear is that in this post-flood world, we are still also in a post-Genesis 3 world, that is, a world where men get drunk, families are split, and curses are uttered. Noah may have been a kind of neo-Adam as well as a prototype of Jesus, but he and his sons were also still caught in the web of evil. Only at the coming of the new and better Noah, Jesus the Christ, would there be true hope and healing for us all, as he hung naked and uncovered atop the cross, drinking the judgment and curse of the Lord down to the very last drop.

The second narrative that tells the sordid tale of humanity's ongoing sin problem is that of the tower of Babel (Gen. 11:1-9). Many ancient cities had a pyramid-shaped worship structure known as a ziggurat, with steps leading up to a shrine at the top. A ziggurat was a manmade mountain that connected earth to heaven. The descendants of Noah, all of whom shared the same language, said, "Come, let us build ourselves a city and a tower with its top in the heavens, and let us make a name for ourselves, lest we be dispersed over the face of the whole earth" (11:4). This attempted ziggurat tower was iconic of people's lust for self-chosen methods of immortality. They wanted to "make a name for themselves," a name that would live on. Here, they could engage in humanity's favorite pastimes: self-salvation projects, immortality inventions, pretending to be gods instead of worshiping the true Lord. And, oh, they did make a name for themselves alright, just not the one they wanted: the place became known as Babel, which is a pun on the Hebrew verb for "confuse, mix, or confound" (balal), for the Lord "confused" their language so that they could no longer work together. More fragmentation of humanity ensued, so that, from Babel, "the LORD dispersed them over the face of all the earth" (11:9).

The shout of this early biblical story echoes all the way down the corridors of the Bible because, in Hebrew, Babel and Babylon are spelled the same. Babylonia would become one of the world's ancient superpowers. The Babylonians would one day crush the people of Israel, demolish their temple, and carry them into exile—to Babylon itself. In Revelation, the last book of the Bible, Babylon is the name given to the world that shakes its fist in God's face and that, like a harlot, seduces the hearts of humanity into evil (e.g., Rev. 14:8; 17:5; 18:1-24). This account in Genesis, therefore, is a microcosm of humanity's dirty future of war against heaven. As the Lord created Eden atop a mountain at the beginning, so thenceforth rebellious humanity will attempt to create our manmade mountains of Eden apart from God, all of which are destined to fail.

So, here we are, eleven chapters into the Bible, and things keep getting worse! People are divided, families in turmoil, and the world's best hope for a "savior" is found inebriated and naked as a jaybird inside his tent. What to do? As we hitchhike into the next section of Genesis, we'll turn down a major highway that we will not exit for a very long time. We might call it the Abraham Interstate. As we shall see, God has a plan, a big and gracious plan, that he is about to set in motion.

Chapter 3

A Half-Brother,
Old Pregnant Woman,
and the Mountaintop Sacrifice

Our ride so far has been very unfunny, but we're in for a belly laugh now. God's about to introduce us to his dry sense of humor. A wrinkled old couple named Abram and Sarai, the last two people we'd expect to be making babies together, are about to conceive a boy whose name, Isaac, means Laughter. We'll drive with them from Mesopotamia to Canaan to Egypt and back again. It's a strange landscape, with odd marriages, removed foreskins, and a near-sacrifice atop a mountain that will reverberate through the rest of the Old Testament story. Onward we go, from Genesis 12-25.

Let's suppose that all we know of the Bible is Genesis 1-11, the section of God's story that we have covered so far. Should the Lord pull us aside to ask, "What do you suggest we do now? Given the mess that the world is in, how should we proceed to get things back on the right track?" what kind of answer might we give? Our common-sense response might be this: "Well, Lord, maybe it's time for a fresh start. How about we find a couple, both young and strong and faithful believers in you, and through them begin a family. This family, as it grows, could provide hope for humanity, be beacons of light in this benighted world." Sounds like a good idea, right? And it is. As we shall see, the Lord does indeed do something along these lines, but also something very much *not* along these lines. In fact, what he does seems destined to fail.

God does select one couple, out of all humanity, to be the epicenter of a new beginning, designed to ripple divine blessings to the entire population. Their names are Abram and Sarai. But young? Hardly. At his last birthday party, the man's cake had so many candles on it, it looked like a fire hazard. He is a whopping seventy-five years "young," and his wife is only ten years his junior. What's more, they've never been called Mom and Dad. And with Sarai's biological clock long having ticked past fertility, there's no possibility of her nursing any babies. And faithful? Wrong again. The father of Abram, a man named Terah, was a worshiper of other gods, so presumably his son was too (Josh. 24:2). And, to accent the weirdness of this couple, Abram and Sarai are half-brother and half-sister, sharing the same father but a different mother (Gen. 20:12). So, as Sarai had been raised alongside Abram in their father's house, she would also have grown up bowing the knee to false deities.

To point out the obvious: this is not a hopeful beginning for humanity's "fresh start."

But the Lord purposefully begins this way to teach us a vital truth about how he operates: he does not tend to work with what we have but with what we do *not* have. In the beginning, he made creation out of nothing. Remember: he "worded" everything into existence. Same here. He takes the "nothing" of this man and woman and makes something great by speaking promise-packed words to them. In the dead womb of Sarai, a son will one day be alive and well. This strange way is God's way of prepping us for the ultimate something-from-nothing miracle: when he takes the dead body of his Son, Jesus, and speaks life back into his corpse so that he rises bodily from the grave. Already in Genesis, therefore, the Father is teaching us about the resurrection of his Son.

As we see from the first part of the Abram and Sarai story, God is also teaching us that he wears no wristwatch, consults no calendar. In other words, he's almost always late—and often laughably, as well as frustratingly, late. When he promises this already aged couple that they will be parents, he does not let Sarai conceive right away. Oh no, that would be too easy. Rather, he forces them to wait not one, not five, not even twenty years. A whopping quarter century passes before Sarai's belly begins to expand with the growth of little Isaac within her. She's ninety when she cuddles her baby boy.

Here, too, the Lord is setting us down in his classroom for an important lesson: when he makes a promise, it shall come to pass, but not according to when *we* think it should. Already in Genesis, therefore, the Father is also teaching us that he will make good on his promise to send that seed or offspring promised to Adam and Eve, the one who will crush the head of humanity's foe. This will happen, however, only according to his timetable.

For the coming of Jesus, the Old Testament people had to wait and wait until they felt as old and lifeless as Sarai's womb. Then, finally, the promised child grew in the most unlikely of places: in the womb of a virgin.

But now to the story itself: what happened? As you might guess, a lot happened, so we will just give some brief sketches of the major episodes. Abram and Sarai pick us hitchhikers up after they've just received the first big shock of their lives: the God—the one true God—whose name is Yahweh, appears to Abram and tells him to pack a suitcase. He and his wife are leaving town for good. The monologue is just too important to leave unquoted.

> Now the LORD said to Abram, "Go from your country and your kindred and your father's house to the land that I will show you. And I will make of you a great nation, and I will bless you and make your name great, so that you will be a blessing. I will bless those who bless you, and him who dishonors you I will curse, and in you all the families of the earth shall be blessed." (Gen. 12:1-3)

Abram, who had grown up an idolater, suddenly has the one true God show up on his doorstep. That would be startling enough. But his words are electrifying: you, Abram, will not only become a nation, numerous and blessed, but *in you the entire human family will be blessed*. Imagine that! This is biblical shorthand for saying that Abram will be what Adam was supposed to be.

What's more, if it's in Abram that all human families are to be blessed, it will be from his family tree that the promised offspring in Genesis 3, the Father's Son, will be born as one of us. A time will come, long down the line, when this single man, Jesus, a descendant of Abram, will be worshiped around the world as the one channel of the Father's blessings to all humanity. For that reason, the New Testament will emphasize that Jesus is the son of this patriarch (Matt. 1:1). In Galatians 3:8, Paul will even say that, when the Lord spoke these words to Abram in Genesis 12, he was preaching the gospel beforehand to him, that is, already announcing the good news of the Savior who is to come, one who would work salvation not only for the physical descendants of Abraham (the Jews), but for the Gentiles as well.

Following the Lord's startling visit and speech, Abram, along with Sarai and their nephew Lot, pulled up stakes and headed for the land named after Canaan, the grandson of Noah (remember him from the last chapter? The one who was cursed?). This rich real estate would be their new home; indeed, it would be the home of their descendants for centuries to come. Abram traveled about from place to place, herding his flocks, as Bedouin people have done for millennia. Everywhere he went, he built altars, which served like little sanctuaries. Little Edens, we might say. Each holy site testified to the fact that Yahweh, the true God, was the owner of this land. Although, by the end of his life, Abram's real estate consisted only of one little plot of ground—a place for family burials—that plot was like a down payment. His grandson, Jacob, would acquire a few more acres. And Jacob's descendants, generations later, would drive out most of the Canaanites to seize possession of the land that God, long before, had sworn to give to Abram.

The adventures and misadventures that Abram and his family endured leave us sometimes shaking our heads, sometimes applauding, and sometimes chuckling. For example, not once but twice, Abram lied to kings about Sarai, claiming that she was his sister (which was partially true), not his wife (which was wholly false). Because she was easy on the eyes, Sarai was added to the king's harem. But, in both cases, the Lord intervened and returned her to Abram. If those occasions reveal the darker, self-serving side of Abram, then the rescue of his nephew Lot from overwhelming enemy forces in Genesis 14 reveals that Abram was also a military man of valor, who knew how to handle a sword and spear. He was also a man of faith who, when the Lord promised him descendants as numerous as the innumerable stars in the sky, "believed the LORD, and he counted it to him as righteousness" (Gen. 15:6).

No sooner, however, do we conclude what a faithful man Abram is before we read that he and Sarai decided that God was inexcusably tardy about providing them with a son. So, they devised their own scheme: at his wife's behest, Abram took her servant, Hagar, to bed and impregnated her as Sarai's surrogate (this was legal back in those days). The child born to them was named Ishmael. Once more, however, the Lord stepped in to say, basically, "Listen, Abram, stick to *my* plan. Ishmael is not the child of promise but a child of old-fashioned procreation. You and your wife will have a son together. Just trust and wait." Then, true to his turtle-paced ways, God made them wait about thirteen more years for this to happen.

About a year or so before the Lord finally delivered on his promise of a baby, two things happened. First,

Abram and Sarai, like newborn babes themselves, got a name—a new name. Henceforth, he who had been Abram was now Abraham, while she who had been Sarai would now be Sarah. Their lives were about to radically change, so their names were altered as well. Second, the Lord had Abraham, as well as every male in his household, undergo a minor surgery. Their foreskins were removed. From that time onward, every male child of Abraham's lineage, at the age of eight days, would be circumcised. Why? For one, this mark in the flesh marked them as members of God's covenant family. If they were not cut in circumcision, they would be cut off from the Lord's people. It was that serious, that vital.

More importantly, since it was through the manhood of Abraham that his sperm (i.e., his seed) would pass into Sarah, who would bear the promised child, this part of his body was marked. This might seem a strange place on the body to bear a divine sign, but Abraham's circumcised flesh was an ongoing, tangible, visual reminder that it would be through his seed that all nations would be blessed. If God is anything, he is the God who loves to use the things of creation, even the sexual member of a man's body, to remind us that we are his own. For Christians, the close equivalent of circumcision is baptism, where Christ uses his Word and water to join us to himself, to make us members of God's new covenant family. Paul writes that believers have experienced "the circumcision of Christ, having been buried with him in baptism" (Col. 2:11-12).

Finally, after twenty-five years of waiting, the long-anticipated son is born! Old Sarah laughs. Everyone around her giggles. The whole scene is so comical, in a divinely humorous sort of way. What else then could they call the child but Yitzchaq, which means "Laughter"? We know him as Isaac. This son of Abraham, this son of promise, is himself a foreshadowing of that Son of Abraham, Son of promise, who is finally to come: Jesus the Christ.

Let's wrap up this chapter with a sober story about this son of Abraham, one whose message was finally and fully understood only when Jesus came as the true Son of Abraham. At some point, probably when Isaac was at least in his teens, if not later, God told him to take Isaac to the land of Moriah and offer him there as a sacrifice (Gen. 22). This is shocking, in and of itself, but when you consider that on Isaac rests the only chance that Abraham's seed will be a blessing to all nations, it is simply incredible. Man of faith that he is, Abraham complies, taking Isaac to Moriah, up the mountain, and even binding him atop the altar. Only at the last instant, while the knife is upraised in Abraham's hand, does God's messenger cry out from heaven to stop the fall of the blade. Abraham had not withheld even his own son from God. In Isaac's place, a ram, whose horns were entangled in a nearby thicket, is offered up as a burnt offering. And once more, the Lord reiterates his promise to Abraham: "In your offspring shall all the nations of the earth be blessed" (Gen. 22:18).

This offspring, this seed by whom all nations are to be blessed, was not Isaac. Nor was it Abraham's grandsons or great-grandsons. This seed or offspring is Jesus, who was anointed by God as the Messiah or Christ. Mount Moriah, where Abraham built his altar, would be the same location where Solomon would later build the temple, where the altar of sacrifice stood (2 Chron. 3:1). Right outside Jerusalem, within sight of Mt. Moriah, this long-awaited Son of Abraham would be bound to the cross with nails, uplifted, and offered as a sacrifice. Rather than a ram being slain in his stead, Jesus, in the stead of all humanity, would be slain. As that ram's horns were entangled in the thicket, Christ, the lamb of God, would be affixed to the cross. Echoing the language of Genesis 22, Paul will tell the Romans, "He who did not spare his own Son but gave him up for us all, how will he not also with him graciously give us all things?" (Rom. 8:32). Abraham's own son was spared, but the Father did not spare his Son. He gave him up for us all, that in him we might receive the blessing of life that God had long before promised to Abraham.

As we stand with Abraham and Isaac atop Mt. Moriah, watching a ram go up in smoke from a burning altar, a ram sacrificed in the place of the promised son, our vista extends for generations to come. We look forward from this mountain to a temple, and finally to a cross, where our salvation story is leading us.

It will take us some time to get there, but as we've learned, we do not worship a Lord who is in any hurry.

Chapter 4

The Heel Man Becomes the God-Fighter and Head of the Chosen Nation

Keep a sharp eye on the character in the driver's seat now. He's not one to turn your back on. This guy could cheat his way through a polygraph test, is the only man in history who crawled into the ring to brawl with God, celebrates four wedding anniversaries every year, and—get this—is the head of the "church" of the Old Testament. To say he's an interesting man is a gross understatement. As we move into Genesis 25, we hitch a ride with Jacob aka Israel. And, wow, what a ride it is.

History, literature, and entertainment have boasted plenty of famous trios. There are the *Three Musketeers*, characters in the classic novel by Alexander Dumas. The slapstick comedians Moe, Larry, and Curly, of the Three Stooges. And Harry, Ron, and Hermione in the *Harry Potter* series. The Bible has trios of its own. In the New Testament, Peter, James, and John are singled out by Jesus on multiple occasions. In the Old Testament, also, we hear about the adventures and misadventures of the trio of patriarchs: Abraham, Isaac, and Jacob.

In the previous chapter, we rode alongside the first two in this trio, old Abe and Isaac, his long-awaited son. Now Isaac is a little different. The Bible focuses more on the fact that he's Abraham's son and Jacob's father than it does on the man himself. No disrespect toward Isaac, but, let's be honest, his name may mean Laughter, but compared to his father and son, he's sort of a yawn. Sure, he has his high moments: he's almost sacrificed (but that narrative is more about Abraham than Isaac), he weds the gorgeous and sly Rebekah (more about her in a moment), and he tries to pass off this wife as his sister (as his dad had done [twice!] with his mom). But all in all, Abraham his father and Jacob his son are more multi-faceted, interesting characters, with longer stories to tell.

We meet Jacob before he's even Jacob; he's an unnamed baby in utero, alongside his twin brother. In this first encounter, we learn something about him that colors the majority of his life: he's a rascally troublemaker. Already in the womb, he's fighting with his brother (Gen. 25:21-23). It's even a race between these siblings to exit the birth canal first. Jacob is born with his tiny fingers clasping his brother's heel, trying, as it were, to yank him back into the womb. In fact, that's how Jacob earns his name: in Hebrew, it's *Ya'aqov*, which means "heel." His brother, who is born first, is covered in red hair. That's how he gets his name, Esau, which is a similar word in Hebrew to "hairy."

So, dear world, meet the brothers Hairy and Heel, Esau and Jacob.

Jacob's life can easily be divided up according to his zip codes. First, his home is in Canaan with Isaac,

Rebekah, and Esau. Second, for two decades, he lives in exile in Mesopotamia, in a place called Haran. There he marries two sister-wives, acquires two co-wives, and begins fathering a passel of kids with these four women. Third, post-exile, he's pitched his tent back home in Canaan. And finally, in his twilight years, he goes into exile once more, this time into Egypt, where he dies at the ripe old age of 147 years (we'll save that for the next chapter). But don't let that seemingly clear, well-delineated outline fool you; Jacob leads a meandering, messed-up life, filled with more downs than ups.

For the first few decades of his life, Jacob is a man on a mission. And that mission is living *down* to his name. *Ya'aqov* ("Heel") is also connected to the Hebrew verb that means grabbing someone by the heels to trip them up, hinder, or betray them. I grew up as a cowboy in New Mexico and Texas, with the pastime of roping steers with my dad and his friends. The "header" roped the steer's horns, and the "heeler" roped the steer's back legs, essentially stopping the animal and often tripping it up. Jacob was a shepherd, not a cowboy, but he was still very much a "heeler." Jacob was intent on "heeling" his older brother, Esau.

Follow the money, and you'll realize what drove Jacob on this heeling crusade. In this ancient society, the oldest son ordinarily received twice the inheritance of his younger brother(s). And, upon the death of the father, the oldest son also became the head of the family. Driven by ambition and greed, deprived at birth from being the eldest, Jacob tried by trickery, manipulation, lying, and backstabbing to reverse this order.

Eventually, he did, in two stages. First, one day when Esau returned from a hunting trip, bone-tired and famished, Jacob said basically, "Tell you what, brother. I'll give you a bowl of soup if you give me your birthright as oldest son." If Jacob bargained selfishly, then Esau agreed stupidly. The exchange was made.

Later, Jacob fully got what he had plotted and schemed to achieve. When Isaac was old and nearly blind, he told Esau to kill a deer, grill him a venison steak, and then he would bless him. This would irrevocably grant Esau the blessing of the firstborn. Isaac's favorite son had always been Esau, while Rebekah's favorite was Jacob. Eavesdropping on this conversation, therefore, sly Rebekah rapidly worked with her son, Jacob, to pull off the first recorded incident of identity theft. Jacob dressed up in his brother's outdoorsy-smelling clothes; his mom covered his hands and neck with goat hair to make him feel like Esau's; then she prepared a meal out of goat that she made to taste like venison (quite the culinary achievement!). When Jacob appeared before his blind father, this younger son lied through his teeth, telling his father that he was Esau. Old Isaac smelled a rat, metaphorically, but also smelled Esau's clothing, literally, so he finally opened his mouth to pronounce the patriarchal blessing. Jacob, the younger son, left the tent with the blessing of the oldest son resting upon him. And, since blessings can't be un-blessed, even when Esau discovered what his brother had done, there was no going back for Isaac. What he had spoken, he had spoken.

Now this might seem to us a highly dysfunctional family mess. And it is. No doubt about it. Brother against brother. Son deceiving father. Wife deceiving husband. Mom and Dad playing favorites. But hidden behind all this is the unseen hand of God, working his will, putting his long-term plan into action. You see, while Esau and Jacob were still in the womb, the Lord had told Rebekah that not only would both boys grow up to be heads of nations, but that there would be a reversal: the older (Esau) would serve the younger (Jacob). We see this over and over in the Bible: on the surface, people seem to be spoiling everything, spreading lies, stealing, hurting, acting egotistically, and rebelling against every good gift of God. And what is God himself doing? Carefully orchestrating events, using weak people and decidedly terrible situations, to bring good out of them and to push his salvation plan forward. So, don't ever imagine that God can't take our worst mess and, in his divine and loving way, bring something good out of it. He's been at that merciful game for as long as humanity's been around.

God's making-treasure-out-of-trash way is evident throughout Jacob's life. Since his brother, Esau, was uttering murderous threats against him, Jacob hightailed it north and east, to the land of his mother's relatives. As he began this long walk, the Lord appeared to him in a grand night vision, complete with the famous "stairway to heaven." He said to Jacob, "I am with you. I will give you this land. I will be with you in exile and bring you back home" (cf. Gen. 28:13-15). Most importantly, the Lord tells Jacob that in his seed or offspring, all the nations of the earth would be blessed. This "offspring" is the one promised to Adam and Eve in Gen. 3:15, the one who would crush the serpent's head. The promise, made to our primal parents, was thus passed down from Adam to Noah to Abraham to Isaac and now to Jacob.

For twenty years, Jacob lived with his mom's relatives in Haran. And what a wild time it was! He fell head-over-heels in love with Rachel; was tricked on their wedding night (because he was drunk?) into sleeping with, and thus become married to, her older sister, Leah; married Rachel a few days later; and, as time went on, took on their maidservants as co-wives. Babies and more babies were born, so that, by the time he left, he was the father of eleven sons and (at least) one daughter. He also became a rich man, with flocks and herds and servants. He left with nothing but the staff in his hand; he headed home as the ancient equivalent of a millionaire CEO. Why? Because he was such a good guy? No, because the Lord, out of sheer mercy, chose to bless him.

When he and his crew were almost back in Canaan, while Jacob was flying solo one night, the Son of God temporarily took on the form of a man and waylaid Jacob. All night, they wrestled. As dawn began to break, the Lord gave Jacob an additional name: he called him, in Hebrew, *Yisra'el*, which means "God-Fighter." Jacob had brawled with God, and God had let him win. This one man, *Yisra'el*—or, as we know him in English, Israel—embodied the people of God who would come from him, the nation of Israel. Their fight, God the Son against Israel, would one day be repeated, in Jerusalem, as the people of God, joined by the Romans, would "brawl" with the Son of God again. They would crucify him, and God would let them win this climactic battle. And, in so doing, he would win for all humanity salvation.

The Lord is never afraid to lose, when it means his children will win what he desired them to have all along.

In the remaining years of his life, Jacob had no chance to settle into relative tranquility in a Florida-type retirement community, where he played golf and sipped martinis. He did reconcile with Esau, who had long ago buried the hatchet and forgiven his twin brother. But it wasn't long before, closer to home, in the lives of own children, things came undone. His daughter was raped and kidnapped. His sons massacred the men in the city where the crime was committed. Jacob made the ridiculous decision of giving the "coat of many colors" to his pet son, Joseph. This precipitated a string of life-altering events, culminating in the brothers selling Joseph into slavery and faking his death to deceive their old father. Jacob might have been given a new name, but he still had his old problems: bad parenting, family turmoil, idiotic decisions, and loads of pain and regret. In other words, Jacob was an awful lot like us, who have a knack for the anti-Midas touch which transforms things into mud and worse.

Yet, just as we do, this patriarch worships the God who's not afraid of mud and muck, who never gives up on even the worst of families, who raises the fallen, heals the wounded, and often does his most hopeful work in our lives when we suppose all hope is lost. We will unpack more of that, as it applies to Jacob, in the next chapter about Joseph, where we will (finally!) exit the Genesis interstate and let our wheels spin down the Exodus highway.

To hitchhike with Jacob is "interesting," to put it mildly! To me, he's one of the most frustrating and captivating individuals in the Bible. Is he a splendid moral example? Hardly. Is he a good father, good husband, good brother and son? One would be hard-pressed to make that argument. But does he believe in the Lord? Yes, for sure. And did the Lord call him, bless him, and use him to pass on the promise of the seed or offspring to come? Yes, indeed!

This fellow, with a stained biography and a fractured family, was the man Israel and the patriarch of the nation of Israel. As such, he was the father of the Old Testament "church," the community of God. The salvation story, which reaches its acme in Jesus, limps along with Jacob. And his limp, much like ours, is no impediment to our Lord's using us, for he specializes in broken and faltering sinners. He is, in fact, not ashamed to be called the Friend of sinners.

Chapter 5

Joseph, the Highly Successful Dead Man

The young man who picks us up in this chapter is barely old enough to drive. He's seventeen. But what Joseph lacks in years, he makes up for in wisdom. An "old soul" we might call him. We are in for a bumpy ride, though, for this young man's life takes quite a downward spiral, only to rocket upward after he's hit rock bottom in Egypt in his 30s. Between his dreams, enslavement, seductions, imprisonment, and political success, Joseph lived a life any storyteller would thrill to recount. So, climb in, and get ready for a road trip that takes us from Canaan to Egypt, and all the way to the finale of Genesis.

When Albert Einstein was a kindergartner, no one said, "See that kid? He'll grow up to be a household name around the world." How could anyone have known? The same could be said for William Shakespeare, Abraham Lincoln, Nelson Mandela, or any renowned leader, author, or athlete. Greatness takes time to emerge. Tom Brady's nickname in fifth grade wasn't the GOAT.

The young man who is the central figure in the closing section of Genesis grew up to greatness; he became the second most powerful man in Egypt. In his case, however, there were some early, faint indicators of the latter heights to which he would one day rise. These indicators came in the form of dreams. In fact, the more you study the Bible, the more you realize just how vital dreams were in God's communication with his people.

When Joseph was the equivalent of a junior in high school, he had twin dreams, one of which involved his brothers (symbolized by sheaves of wheat) bowing down to him, the other of which had his brothers *and parents* (symbolized by the sun, moon, and stars) bowing before him. When he had these dreams and relayed them to his family, they probably seemed as strange to him as they were odious to his brothers. But, in a short time, these dreams appeared to be nothing more than a foolish boy's fancy, as Joseph's life devolved into a waking nightmare.

What happened? Well, jealousy, hatred, malice, lies, and kidnapping happened. In the last chapter, we mentioned the dozen or so children that Jacob was fathering through his mini-harem of four wives. But we skipped over one crucial detail: Jacob's favorite, beloved wife was Rachel. Now Rachel only had two babies, both boys: Joseph and Benjamin (during the birth of the latter, the mother died). Because he was the older son of the chosen wife, Joseph was also Daddy's favorite. The whole family knew how he doted on him. And if there were any lingering doubts, those vanished when Jacob presented Joseph with a fancy suit of clothing (traditionally translated as "the coat of many colors"). Now, you might be thinking, "Wait! Didn't Jacob's own mom and dad play favorites too?" Ah, yes, they did; Isaac loved Esau, while Rebekah loved Jacob. But one generation repeating the same mistakes as their parents—a modern reality with which we are all too familiar—is as old as the hills. There's nothing new under the sun.

We don't need to be prophets to forecast that Joseph's siblings were not going to shrug their shoulders at their father's preferential treatment. That look-at-me garment the teenager sported, plus his two dreams of supposed future superiority over them—not to mention the fact that he shoved those dreams in their faces *by making sure they knew about his dreams*—well, all this pushed Joseph's brothers over the proverbial edge. They didn't just look down on their kid brother or pick on him; they hated his guts. In fact, so hot was their rage that they came close to murdering him.

So began Joseph's slow and painful death. The word "death" might seem extreme, but it's the best word to encapsulate the next several years of his life. No, Joseph didn't end up a corpse, but it was like important pieces of his identity were daily chopped off and dropped into the grave: his connection to family; his homeland; his good name; his freedom. Every time we think things can't possibly get worse for him, they do. In fact, his youthful dreams seem to become, in hindsight, a sort of deceptive mockery. Rather than being someone to whom others bow down, he himself is bowed down by betrayal, chains, false accusation, and incarceration. In the language of the New Testament, Joseph acquired a PhD in "taking up his cross and following Jesus." But, as we've seen in previous chapters, in the shadowland of his people's suffering, the Lord of light was at work secretly, using the rubble of human despair to construct a vast edifice of hope.

The first episode of Joseph's years-long death was kicked off when Jacob sent him to check up on his brothers, who were shepherding the family's sheep. No sooner did he show up in their camp before they seized him, ripped off his loathsome robe, and chunked him into a deep pit for safekeeping. Some wanted to slit his throat and be done with "the dreamer"; the oldest brother (Reuben) wanted to spare him. In the end, brother Judah's suggestion won the day: he proposed they sell Joseph as a slave to a caravan of traders who were passing by. And so they did. For a few pieces of silver, they sold their own flesh and blood. Then, adding an extra layer of diabolical disgust to their deeds, they took Joseph's robe, splashed goat blood all over it, and sent it to their father as "evidence" that his beloved, favorite, teenage son had been ripped to shreds by a wild beast. Jacob, who had deceived his father, was himself deceived by his own sons. Heartbroken, choking on despair, this dad sank into a midnight sorrow that only a parent who has buried a child can comprehend.

And Joseph? He stepped into a strange labyrinth of life, where, behind every corner, he didn't know if he'd face the smile of an approving master or the roar of a hungry lion. He wound up in Egypt, with the caravan of traders to whom he had been sold. There, they in turn sold him to an official of Pharaoh named Potiphar. At first, Joseph wowed everyone, especially his boss. If father Jacob was a Heel, then son Joseph was a Head. And, soon enough, Potiphar elevated him to be the head or overseer of the entire house. What was the secret to Joseph's success, even as a slave? It was no secret at all:

"The LORD was with Joseph, and he became a successful man…the LORD caused all that he did to succeed in his hands" (Gen. 37:2-3). Outwardly, Joseph was enslaved, but inwardly, he was the Lord's freeman: free to work hard, wisely, sacrificially, faithfully, and successfully, despite being ripped away from everything he had once known.

Just as Joseph's life was (sort of) coming together, it fell apart. Again. We are told that Joseph was a handsome and well-built young man. Easy on the eyes, as we say. And the eyes of Potiphar's wife were definitely checking him out. It wasn't long before she tried to coax him into her bed. He refused. She tried again. He refused. She persisted. And he kept saying no. Finally, one day, Potiphar's wife grabbed Joseph's clothes and said, "Have sex with me!" When he ran away from her grasping hands, he left behind his outer garment. This spurned woman then, like Joseph's brothers, used his clothing as "evidence." She told her husband that the Hebrew servant had sexually assaulted her and, when she screamed, he fled, leaving behind his clothes. Furious, Potiphar threw Joseph into prison. From son to slave, from slave to (falsely accused) criminal, from criminal to an inmate in an Egyptian dungeon, down and still farther down went Joseph.

Joseph's "rock bottom" was here, in prison. But it was also here, in time, that his long descent became a rapid ascent, his "death" a "resurrection." As he had in Potiphar's house, so in this house of bondage, Joseph stood out as an especially gifted young man. Why? The same reason as before: "the LORD was with Joseph and showed him steadfast love" (Gen. 39:21). This is a necessary reminder to us that hard times in the lives of believers are not evidence that the Lord has abandoned us or no longer loves us. These are seasons of refinement and testing. Our Father is making us less that he might be more within us; draining us of ego so that the void might be filled with himself. So it is with us; so it was with Joseph. Soon, the head of the prison, observing Joseph's gifts, put him in charge of all the prisoners.

At this juncture, the theme of dreams reemerges in the narrative—reemerges in a huge way. Two of Joseph's fellow inmates, both former servants of Pharoah, have dreams, which Joseph correctly interprets. One of these, the cupbearer, when he is released and once more assumes his position in service to the king, eventually becomes the key to unlock the door to Joseph's future.

Here's what happens. One night, Pharaoh has two troubling dreams (you see, don't you, how often "twos" or "twins" keep emerging in this story?). He's so upset by these dreams that he summons all his magicians, his wise men, but not a soul can interpret the dreams. Finally, stepping forth, the cupbearer chimes in to say, basically, "Hey, King, I know a guy." That "guy," of course, is our friend Joseph.

With a speed that must have been shocking, Joseph is ushered out of prison, gets a shower and shave, stands before the royal court, listens to the king's two dreams, and provides a precise interpretation: a famine, a devouring seven-year famine, is barreling toward Egypt. Astonished and impressed by Joseph's wisdom, as well as his proposed plans for famine-prepping, the king designates Joseph his vice-regent on the spot. In a whopping 24-hour period, this prisoner is raised from death to life, from pit to pinnacle. In this way, Joseph is an archetype of Jesus himself, a picture of death and resurrection.

The chapters in Genesis that summarize the next few years are full of action and emotion. Preparations kick off. The famine sets in. And things get bad, starvation bad, in all surrounding countries. Like a single oasis in the desert, Egypt alone has food. And, one memorable day, which hungry family shows us in Joseph's court? Which band of brothers bows down before him? Like a dream come true (literally!), there are the long-lost siblings of Joseph, taking a knee before him. Only they haven't a clue that this "Egyptian" is their kid brother. He's well into his thirties now; they last saw him when he was seventeen. He looks, talks, and acts like an Egyptian prince.

The drama that ensues is some riveting reading. Joseph puts his brothers through some hard tests to discover if they're still the unfraternal backstabbers they were almost two decades prior. When the fourth oldest brother, Judah, the very one who had devised the scheme to sell him into slavery, acts selflessly, putting his own life on the line, Joseph makes his decision. In a jaw-dropping moment, he reveals his true identity, "I am your brother, Joseph!" Though initially stunned— how could they not be?—the brothers embrace Joseph, they all weep, and soon plans are underway for all of Joseph's family, including his old father, Jacob, to be relocated to Pharaoh's land, where there is food aplenty.

In the last few chapters of Genesis, as Jacob's large family pulls up stakes and settles in Egypt, father and son hug in a tearful reunion. Jacob had thought Joseph was dead the whole time that God was using Joseph to save Jacob's, and everyone else's, lives. Oh, the divine irony. This irony of the Lord's mysterious, hidden, slow ways of working in this world is one of the major themes of Joseph's life.

Joseph will explain it this way to his brothers, "God sent me before you to preserve for you a remnant on earth, and to keep alive for you many survivors. So it was not you who sent me here, but God" (45:7-8). Later, he will say it this way, "As for you, you [my brothers] meant evil against me, but God meant it for good, to bring it about that many people should be kept alive, as they are today" (50:20).

All those years that Joseph was enduring a kind of living death, unbeknownst to him at the time, the Lord was preparing him to keep people alive.

This is crucial for understanding the God of the Bible: if you want to see him at work, pluck out your eyeballs and stick them in your ears. That's how one of my teachers Kenneth Korby expressed it. And how true it is. What do we see Joseph going through? Betrayal, chains, false accusation, imprisonment, degradation. But what do we hear? The Lord is with him, he loves him, he is blessing him. Only after Joseph's "resurrection" does everything begin to make sense. We have to put our eyeballs in our ears, that is, to see by hearing, to view God's activity in this world by what he speaks instead of the contradictory realities before our eyes.

All of this prepares us for how our Father is at work in the life of Jesus, whom we can think of as the Greater Joseph. Especially in the death of Jesus, what do our eyes see? Betrayal, whips, nails, false accusation, degradation, spit, mockery, and lots and lots of blood. There hangs a condemned man, naked and gasping for breath, executed publicly. Our eyes say: He is a failure, a loser, a lost cause. But our eyes lie. Our ears tell the truth, for we have heard from him that his crucifixion is the way he shows his glory. His defeat is a victory over sin. While he hangs there naked, he is clothing the world with love. After Jesus' resurrection, all of this begins to make sense as Christ opens the minds of his disciples to see how it was all foretold in the Old Testament.

Let's ask Joseph to pull the car over so we can hop out of this chapter, but let's do so by noting one final, but by no means minor, detail. At the end of his life, Jacob spoke prophetic words about each of his sons. Of Judah, his fourth-born, he said that the promised seed, the Messiah, would come from his line (49:8-12). From his tribe would arise the King, whom the Bible later calls "the Lion of the tribe of Judah" (Rev. 5:5). We will return to this in a later chapter, so tuck it away for now. The promise of Jesus is still there, still moving forward, still unfolding in God's long and faithful salvation story.

Chapter 6

Burning Bushes and Split Seas

I know what you've been thinking: Dang, are we ever going to leave Genesis in our rear-view mirror? Well, now we finally have. But we needed to hitchhike our way slowly through that book because, in a sense, the entire Bible rests on those opening narratives. We could call the remainder of the Scriptures "Genesis, Continued." Behind the wheel of the vehicle that picks us up at the boundary of Genesis and Exodus is a weathered, bearded man. He will drive us to the end of Deuteronomy and drop us off at the border of the promised land. And he is, hands down, one of the top three most important people in all human history. Friends, meet Moses.

Stop the average person on the street today and ask them, "What's one word you associate with Egypt?" My hunch is that nine out of ten people would say, "Pyramids." But if you stopped the average Israelite on the streets of Jerusalem to ask, "What's one word you associate with Egypt?" I bet nine (or ten!) out of ten would say, "Slavery." We hear "Egypt" and think

"Wow!" but they heard "Egypt" and thought "Woe." They remembered crippling, dehumanizing chains.

At the heart of the confession of the Israelites, in the very words that preface the Ten Commandments, God says to his people, "I am the LORD your God, who brought you out of the land of Egypt, out of the house of slavery" (Exod. 20:2). That is the baseline confession of who God is for Israel. And if the liberating Lord is at the center of their belief, then also at the center is the man by whom God brought about this merciful deliverance: Moses.

Moses made it easy for us to remember the basic threefold outline of his bio. From infancy to the age of forty, he lived in Egypt as an adopted member of the royal household. From forty to eighty, he lived in the remote wilderness with his wife's family, where he was a shepherd. And from eighty to one hundred twenty, he was the rescuer, leader, and teacher of Israel as they wandered through the desert. While we know a few details about those first eighty years, we have a whopping four books of material about the final four decades of his life. Those four books are Exodus, Leviticus, Numbers, and Deuteronomy. Together with Genesis, these five books are known by the Hebrew name Torah (which means "teaching") or the Greek name Pentateuch ("five books").

When we were dropped off in the last chapter, everything was going gangbusters for the people of God. Joseph was the Egyptian equivalent of the Vice President. Pharaoh gave managerial jobs to Joseph's brothers. And the extended family settled in a section of Egypt called Goshen. There, the husbands and wives began making lots and lots of babies, so the original seventy members of Jacob's family who arrived in Egypt expanded exponentially. Israel got big. And, over time, Israel also got noticed—and not in a good way.

Listen to these ominous words: "Now there arose a new king over Egypt, who did not know Joseph" (Exod. 1:8). What he did know—or at least thought he knew—was that these Hebrews posed a threat to national security. What if an enemy attacked Egypt and the non-native Israelites allied with the invaders? What then? So the government launched a series of events calculated to weaken and demoralize Israel. Enslavement? Yes. Hard labor? Yes. Enforced infanticide of male Israelites? Tragically, yes. All newborn males were to be thrown into the Nile.

Here, Moses steps onto the biblical stage. When he was born, his mother hid him for three months, then set him afloat in the Nile inside a little wicker basket (called in Hebrew an "ark"). He was discovered by Pharaoh's daughter, who named and adopted him. Little did Pharaoh realize the boy raised under his roof would one day bring that roof down on Egypt.

Here, as elsewhere, we see God laboring in his slow and muted way. Moses would have been educated. He would have observed the conduct of Egyptian leaders. This boy, who would grow up to write five books of the Bible and lead the Israelites, would put into practice what the Lord, in his divine ingenuity, had made possible. God arranged to have the enemy orchestrate their own future demise. In a similar way, Jesus would be attacked, arrested, tried, and put to death, just like all the powers of hell wanted to happen. And as it happened, in Christ's death, he destroyed death, demolished sin, and crushed the head of the Serpent beneath his heel. Evil is always falling into the pits it digs with its own hands.

When he was about forty years old, Moses killed an Egyptian who was beating an Israelite slave. Then away he ran from the long arm of the law, on the lam for four decades in the water-poor, sand-rich waste of the Sinai peninsula. He married a local woman named Zipporah. He fathered two sons. He cared for his father-in-law's flocks. No doubt it was a simple life. Maybe Moses was content to go on eking out a living in these arid boon-docks. He had been a Somebody for forty years and was a relative Nobody for the next forty years. He would ease into his twilight years, just being an average Joe. And so it might have been, had not God showed up on his doorstep—or, rather, in a burning bush—with a huge job for this octogenarian.

In the Old Testament, the Father often sent his Son as a messenger (in Hebrew, *malak*) to deliver a command or word of comfort to his people. English translations unfortunately render *malak* as "angel," so keep in mind it simply means "messenger." In other words, don't confuse the divine Christ with a created angel! To Moses, the Father sent Jesus as a messenger. He appeared at a mountain called Horeb and Sinai (same place, different names), inside a mysterious fiery bush, with a herculean task for this shepherd. He was to retrace his steps to Egypt, tell Pharaoh to sign an emancipation proclamation for the Israelites, and shepherd God's people back to this same mountain and then onward to the land of Canaan, where Abraham and Isaac had lived. In other words, the Lord was send-ing Moses on (what seemed to be) Mission Impossible.

After Moses blathered out a long string of excuses as to why he was Mr. Wrong for this job, he finally surrendered to the Lord's ironclad will. During this same conversation, God's Son also gave to Moses his personal name, Yahweh (English translations will print this name in all caps as "LORD" to distinguish it from other Hebrew titles written as "Lord"). Then Moses, with his older brother Aaron, as his sidekick, trekked to Egypt.

Now in those days, the Pharaoh was not considered just a powerful man; he was deemed a god. Talk about a recipe for arrogance! And, sure enough, this big-headed "god," when Moses and Aaron relayed Yahweh's message to him, not only gave them a snarling "No!" but punished the enslaved Israelites for even wanting their freedom. This, in turn, kicked off a war: it was Yahweh vs. the gods of the Egyptians.

As you might have guessed, the Egyptian deities, including Pharoah, were soon beaten black and blue by the Lord's almighty fist. These blows were struck through ten plagues, everything from the Nile becoming blood to frogs infesting the land and, finally, the death of the oldest son in every Egyptian family. With that last plague, God kicked off what would become the annual springtime celebration called Passover (named after the Lord "passing over" [sparing] the firstborn sons of his people). A lamb was sacrificed, its blood daubed on the Israelite doors, and its body cooked and eaten, along with unleavened bread and bitter herbs. The people of God thus ate the body of the lamb sacrificed for them, whose blood protected them. In this way, the Passover lamb prefigured Jesus, whom John the Baptist calls "the Lamb of God, who takes away the sin of the world" (John 1:28). And Jesus, this Lamb, on Passover night,

gave bread to his disciples and said, "Take, eat; this is
my body" (Matt. 26:26). In the Lord's Supper, therefore,
the church eats the body of the Lamb sacrificed on the
cross for us, whose blood covers us to make us right in
God's eyes.

During Passover night, as the wails of griev-
ing Egyptian families pierced the night, hardhearted
Pharaoh finally relented. After centuries of captivity,
the Israelites were free! Laden with their own goods,
along with Egyptian treasuries, they sallied forth toward
a new land, a new hope swelling within their hearts. But
no sooner had they put some miles between them and
Egypt than the king reneged on his promise. Maybe he
got to thinking in dollar signs about how he had just
lost his nation's free labor supply. So, summoning his
troops, he chased down the Israelites, trapping them
at the edge of the Red Sea (more precisely, in Hebrew,
Yam Suf, the Sea of Reeds).

At that body of water, the Lord of Israel showed
his people that the entire duty of saving and redeeming them rested solely on his broad shoulders. By a
strong east wind, blowing all night, he split the sea so
all Israel strolled where fish had been swimming, with
liquid walls raised to their right and left. Then, when
the Egyptian army, with the king at their head, got the
harebrained idea of following the people of God, the
walls became waves, falling to crush and drown the foe.
The Egyptians, who had drowned Israelite babies in the
Nile were themselves drowned in the water of the sea,
while God's people passed safely through.

Israel learned an everlasting lesson that day: the
Lord uses water in two ways, to kill and make alive, to
save and destroy. When Jesus gave his church the water

of baptism—a kind of mini "Red Sea"—that lesson took on added importance. In baptism, our "old Egyptian self," our sinful nature, is drowned and a new person, a new nature, recreated in Jesus, emerges from the other side of that baptismal sea. Baptism transforms us from Egyptians into Israelites.

As the Lord's people, under Moses, left the Red Sea to journey toward the mountain where God had appeared in the burning bush, they slogged their way through a bleak and barren landscape. Picture a place like Death Valley in the United States. Mouths dried. Stomachs growled. And bellyaching began. Despite the baseless rumors you might have heard, God in the Old Testament is not a bloodthirsty, tyrannical monster who is always flying off the handle in divine temper tantrums that leave scores of corpses littering the ground. He is gracious. He is merciful. And he is—to use the Hebrew idiom—"long-of-nose," that is, patient. Case in point: he did not react to the Israelites' bellyaching with brain-smashing. Instead, beginning then and continuing until they reached the land of promise, he became their traveling chef and water-giver. A tasty, miraculous carbohydrate appeared on the ground, which the Israelites named "manna" (which, in Hebrew, humorously means "What is it?"). This mysterious food became their daily bread. And, whenever they needed water, Moses took his staff—the same staff with which he had deprived Egypt of water by turning the Nile into blood—and with that staff brought forth potable water for Israel from a large stone. Paul later wrote that "they drank from the spiritual Rock that followed them, and the Rock was Christ" (1 Cor. 10:4). The rock fountain, in other words, was just the outward mask for the true source of their ongoing life: the Son of God. He never deserted Israel, but followed them and, indeed, led them as their guardian and provider.

About three months after leaving Egypt, the Israelites put down stakes at Mt. Sinai, where they would remain camped for a little over a year. About fifty-eight Bible chapters (from Exodus 19-40, through all of Leviticus, and until Numbers 10) document what happened at this mountain. This means that about one-third of the Torah recounts teachings, revelations, events, and constructions at Sinai. That fact leaves no doubt that this is crucial material.

In a variety of ways, what is said and done at Sinai will be quoted, alluded to, repurposed, re-lived, and celebrated for the remainder of the Bible. For instance, in a Moses-kind-of-way, the prophet Elijah will visit Sinai, where God will appear to him as he appeared to Moses and all Israel. Christ's famous "Sermon on the Mount" intentionally imitates Moses' "Sermon on the (Sinai's) Mount." The tabernacle, built at Sinai, will become the model for the later temple and, eventually, for the true sanctuary of God: the body of Jesus, the Word of God, who became flesh and "tabernacled" among us (John 1:14). We might put it this way: at Sinai was all the raw material out of which later teachings, practices, festivals, sacrifices, sanctuaries, prophecies, psalms, and more were constructed for Israel.

Most importantly, at Mount Sinai, the Lord made a covenant with Israel. This covenant—sometimes called the "Sinai covenant" or the "covenant of the law" or merely "the old covenant"—was based on the Lord's choice of Israel, his detailed outline of how they were to live in this world, and what means he provided for their ongoing cleansing and the atonement of their sins. And this is so very crucial: *this covenant was temporary.* The laws were never, and could never, be kept perfectly. The sacrifices were never, and could never, fully atone for Israel. What happened at Sinai was preparatory for what would happen in the life and ministry of Jesus. He would perfectly keep the law for us. He would offer the perfect sacrifice for us. And he would give us the new and better covenant, based entirely upon his work, his offering, his obedience, his grace for us.

Since we will be parked at Sinai for more than a year, let's turn off the engine and step out of the car onto the hot desert sand. For the time being, we will step away from Moses and hang out with Aaron, his brother, to see what he can teach us about tents, sacrifices, and the priesthood.

Chapter 7

Blood, Fire, and Sanctuary

In this chapter, we are parked in the shadow of Mt. Sinai. The engine's off. So, for a change, let's lean on the hood beside this fellow who's decked out in some odd-looking regalia. He also has blood on his hands. Goat blood. Ox blood. Sacrificial blood. His name is Aaron, and he's the brother of Moses. He's also high priest #1 in Israel. Aaron is going to help us sort through all this material about clean and unclean, holy ground, animal sacrifices, and some other matters that seem bizarre to us.

Whether you're cracking open the Bible for the first time or you've been poring over it for years, chances are you do plenty of head scratching when you get to the latter half of Exodus, with all this talk of blueprints for the tabernacle. And Leviticus? Forget it. That book makes as much sense in English as it would in hieroglyphics. Why all the sacrifices? Why the tabernacle? Why priests? I get it. To us, it is weird stuff. But, once you wrap your mind around a few facts, it's also fascinating stuff. In various and surprising ways, these books escort us down the path to Jesus. The light of Exodus and Leviticus shines on Christ, illuminating his ministry and mission.

First, in these biblical books, you'll read plenty about "clean" and "unclean." To help us understand these two categories, let's use an example. Suppose I ask you to spit into a cup and drink it. You would say, "No! That's gross." But pause to consider this: what do you do unconsciously all day long? You swallow the saliva that is in your mouth. So what's the difference between swallowing the saliva in your mouth and the saliva in the cup? Simple: one is *inside* you and the other has passed *outside* the border of your body. Or consider this example: none of us looks at another person and thinks, "That person has blood and urine and feces inside them—how disgusting!" Of course not. But, if we see their blood, urine, or (especially) feces outside their body, that does bother us, right? Why? For the same reason: what's inside is fine but what's outside the border of the body is not. We might put it this way: what's inside is "clean" but what's outside is "unclean." What distinguishes the two is a border or line that's been crossed.

In the world of ancient Israel, borders or lines were everywhere. Some things (like pigs) were always over the border into unclean. Other things (like the holy objects in the sanctuary) were always inside the border of clean. And still other things (people in particular) were crisscrossing the lines: sometimes clean, sometimes unclean. For instance, when a woman was on her period, she was temporarily unclean, as was a man after he had a discharge of semen. But when these people underwent a washing or changed their clothes (or both), they crossed the border back into clean again.

The average Israelite, therefore, moved between these borders of ritual cleanness and uncleanness their whole lives. The laws given to Israel at Mt. Sinai described where these ritual borders lay. It was the duty of the Israelites, especially the priests, to understand these borders and the means that God had provided for his people to become clean again.

Second, there's a lot of talk about holiness in Exodus and Leviticus. Why? In Israel, only God was holy by nature. Holiness was utterly entwined in his God-ness. But the Lord desired to *share his holiness*, to gift it to people, places, things, and times. For instance, the seventh day, the Sabbath, was a holy time. The altar was a holy thing. The tabernacle was a holy place. Israel was a holy nation. Their holiness was real, but it was also "on loan" from the holy God. Should he wish, he could also un-holy something. He did this, for instance, in Ezekiel's day when the temple became so defiled by false gods that the Lord vacated the sanctuary. When he did, every bit of holiness disappeared with him; the temple became just another building, no more or less sacred than a cowshed.

The crucial point is this: holiness was primarily about being close to God—as in *spatially* close to him. While Israel was at Sinai, the Lord gave Moses highly detailed instructions on how to build him a special tent, called a "tabernacle." It had two rooms. The inner one was the Holy of Holies (also translated "Most Holy Place") and the outer one was the Holy Place. When the tabernacle was completed, God moved into the Holy of Holies. Though he was still everywhere present in creation, he was *especially there* for Israel. He located himself in that room for his people's sake, to be close to them, to reside in their midst. And because the holy Lord was there, it was the holiest place in the world. This also meant that the closer anything or anyone was to that room, the holier they were. Holiness or sanctity, therefore, was about proximity to the holy Lord in the Holy of Holies.

Are you with me so far? We have clean and unclean. We have holiness. But we also have a big, ugly, looming problem: sin. The Lord was well aware that his people were imperfect mortals, who would break his commands in what they desired, thought, spoke, did, and left undone. As a righteous God, he would not wink at or shrug off their wrongdoing. Rather, their sins had to be covered and taken away. Someone or something had to pay the price. Theoretically, the Lord could have devised a system whereby the sinners themselves paid for their sins. They could shed a little blood or a lot of blood for their misbehavior, depending on its severity, and thereby earn forgiveness by paying the penalty in themselves.

But that is not how God operates. Instead, he laid out a complete system of sacrifices, in which goats, lambs, cattle, and birds shed their blood to atone for the sins of the Israelites. *The Lord devised a system of sacrificial substitution in which forgiveness and cleansing were obtained by something else dying for the sinner.* The blood of these animals was shed, and their bodies were burned upon the altar as the ongoing, God-ordained way that his people would continue to have access to him. Knowing this explains so much about the min-istry of Jesus, especially the shedding of his blood and his sacrificial death by crucifixion. He was, as John the Baptist called him, "the Lamb of God who takes away the sin of the world" (John 1:29). He was our substitute; he became our sin.

We might say, therefore, that written upon the cross is the whole text of Leviticus; that is its background.

As these sacrifices were offered, who would take care of the altar, the blood, the sanctuary, and everything in it? Who would perform all the rituals, teach the people, lead worship? For these duties, the Lord chose one of the twelve tribes of Israel, the Levites (descendants of Jacob and Leah's third-born son, Levi). And from this tribe, he selected one clan, the descendants of Aaron. So, Aaron, his sons, his grandsons, and so on, throughout the generations, were set aside to serve as priests. They had spatial access to God in a way that others did not. Think of it this way: if you visit Washington D.C., you can see the White House from a distance; you might even be fortunate enough to get a tour of it. But unless you are invited to do so for some special reason, you cannot stroll into the Oval Office. The same would be true for the Vatican or even the headquarters of a Fortune 500 company. Not everyone has the same access to the same places. There is no democratizing of space.

In the tabernacle, every priest could serve in the forecourt, the area immediately in front of the sanctuary, where the altar was located. The priests took turns entering the Holy Place to care for the lights on the menorah or to burn incense on a small altar. But only the high priest could enter the inner sanctum, the Holy of Holies, and he did this only once a year, on a special day called Yom Kippur ("Day of Atonement"). Just like we learned about ritual borders regarding clean and unclean, this was a *spatial border*. Who could get closest to the presence of God? The high priest. Who was next closest? Regular priests. Who next? A group called the Levites, who were the priests' servants and helpers. And who next? Common Israelites. Thus, if you were not a descendant of Aaron, not of the tribe of Levi, but just an average man or woman in Israel, there was absolutely no way you could ever, or would ever, enter the tabernacle itself, much less the Holy of Holies. You had to be satisfied with being at a spatial distance from the holiest spot in the world, wherein God was enthroned.

Once again, Leviticus provides the colorful hues and tones in the picture of the new and better gift that Jesus gives to us. Christ was the walking, talking, flesh-and-blood, human tabernacle of God. His body is the new and everlasting sanctuary. That means that to be near him is to be near the Holy of Holies. And to whom was Jesus near? He was called the Friend of Sinners. No one was ever "not good enough" or "not holy enough" or "not priestly enough" to be in his presence. Jesus demolished the spatial borders between high priest, regular priest, Levite, and ordinary Israelite. All were welcome to stand in the healing shadow of his sanctity. What's more, the New Testament tells us that, when Jesus died, he entered the *heavenly* Holy of Holies as our new and better high priest. He thus opened up the way for us, in him, to enter the presence of our Father. This means that when we become part of the body of Jesus in baptism, we have the status of high priests.

Another feature of Exodus and Leviticus to note is that God planned out their year for them. Just like we have our calendar year, with its holidays and special observances, Israel had a year punctuated with holy days and weeks. Every seventh day (Saturday) was a Sabbath.

Three major festivals were observed, two in the spring and early summer (Passover and Weeks [Pentecost]), and one in the fall (Tabernacles). Also in the fall was the day I mentioned before, Yom Kippur, which was the most solemn day of the year, in which all Israelites fasted, animals were sacrificed, their blood sprinkled inside the Holy of Holies, the high priest confessed the sins of the nation, and a goat (traditionally translated "scapegoat") carried off those sins into the wilderness. Divinely baked into the rhythm of Israel's year were these festivals, and this fast, to keep before their eyes the remembrance of who they were and what God had done, and continued to do, for them.

This calendar year also helps to map the ministry of Jesus. His arrest, death, and resurrection took place during Passover week, for he brings us from slavery to freedom, from death to life. His crucifixion is also the final Yom Kippur, for in his death, once and for all, he atoned for the sins of the world. In Jesus, we enter an unending Sabbath, for we rest in him and his mercy. His body is our tabernacle, where we dwell with God, in an ongoing celebration of Tabernacles. And on Weeks or Pentecost itself, Jesus sent his Holy Spirit upon his followers in Acts 2.

The more we are able to discern the significance of the Old Testament holy days, the more we will also see how God, from Mt. Sinai onward, was having his people "practice" reception of the gifts that were to arrive in Jesus Christ. The Israelite calendar, therefore, looked back to what God had done for his people, looked presently at what he continued to do for them, and looked forward to the days and weeks and years of the Messiah, when he would tear the final page off that Israelite calendar and replace it with himself.

As you read through Exodus and Leviticus, there will be plenty of material that seems odd, even disconcerting, to you. And that's okay. I've been studying and teaching about these books for about thirty years, and I'm still learning new things every day. That is one of the joys of the Bible! Long ago, a rabbi said of the Torah, "Turn it, turn it, for everything is in it." When we pick up the Scriptures and turn them this way, then that way, new treasures and insights keep dropping out of these pages.

Now we need to wrap up this brief pit stop at Sinai. Time to load up, start the engine, and get rolling again. Onward we go!

Chapter 8

Forty Years of Waiting and Wandering in the Wilderness

After our one-chapter stop with Aaron, it's time to hit the road again with his kid brother, Moses. We'll also be hitting a painful and disappointing dead-end at the border of the promised land. There, we'll be forced to put the car in reverse, turn around, and begin a long and circuitous route that will drag on for forty years in the wilderness. At the end, Moses will sing his swan song and, standing beside this 120-year-old man, we'll lift our eyes to gaze at the horizon, into the land flowing with milk and honey.

Have you heard the crazy story about the guy who was head-over-heels in love with a girl, married her, but then she cheated on him during their honeymoon? Yes, their honeymoon. But that newlywed affair was only the beginning of a long list of wedded woes. Over the next four decades of marriage, things went from bad to worse. She grumbled nonstop about how little he cared for her, how much better her life had been before they spoke their vows, and how she didn't trust him. What's more, not content with the honeymoon fling, she became a serial adulteress, stepping out on him again and again. Shockingly, through this all, he still loved her. He forgave her. He was a faithful and selfless provider. Do you know this story? If not, when you read Exodus 32 through the end of Deuteronomy, you will. Because the "guy" is the Lord, and his "girl" is Israel. This is the narrative of Yahweh and Israel's forty years of wedded un-bliss.

You see, one way to envision what happened at Sinai is a marriage ceremony. The divine groom slipped a wedding ring on lady Israel's finger at the Sinai Chapel. A covenant was made and sealed between the two. Their honeymoon was long, about a year. During those months, much of what we discussed in the last chapter happened: the tabernacle was erected; Aaron and his sons became priests; God taught Israel the Ten Commandments and lots of other rules and regulations for how to conduct themselves and organize their society. We might say that Israel discovered how to be a faithful, holy, loving, and serving bride to her heavenly Husband.

She also had barely hung up her wedding dress before she hopped into bed with another god. While Moses was on the peak of Sinai, receiving instructions from the Lord, the Israelites were down below, slumming with idolatry. They urged Aaron to make them a god, specifically, a visual symbol of a deity. He evidently didn't need much arm-twisting, because lickety-split, he went to work to mold a "golden calf." In the ancient Near East, bulls or calves were often used as images for, or platforms for, a deity. This calf was in gross, direct violation of God's prohibition to Israel. In fact, in the aftermath, the Lord was so furious with his people that were it not for Moses' intercession, all Israel would have been stomped out of existence. But God relented and forgave. Israel was spared and given another chance to act with fidelity.

That chance soon came. Leaving their camp at Sinai, the Israelites began the trek toward the land that God had sworn to give Abraham, Isaac, and Jacob. Remember that Jacob and his family had migrated from this country during a famine, centuries before. The whole time they were living in Egyptian exile—during the good years, the bad years, and the very ugly slavery years—they had been awaiting a return. Now was their chance. They had good leaders. They had a sanctuary and priests. And, last but certainly not least, they had the Creator of heaven and earth on their side, with a resumé replete with salvation achievements, all done on behalf of Israel.

Right away, though, there were dire signs of a looming catastrophe. Among the people, grumbling gave way to accusation, accusation to revolt, and revolt was squashed by plagues that took the lives of many of the Israelites. Bearing the burden of leadership, Moses became so overwhelmed that he asked God to put him out of his misery. As if this weren't enough, Moses' own siblings became his slanderers. His brother and sister, Aaron and Miriam, gave a thumbs down to his choice of Mrs. Moses. Then, they became spiritually uppity and started trash-talking their brother. These were markers of a splintering community.

The negativity spiked at the border of Canaan. Moses sent out a dozen spies to reconnoiter the land. Forty days later, they returned. All but two of them

(Joshua and Caleb) basically said, "Oh, yeah, it's a fat and rich land, but we don't stand a chance. The cities are impregnable. And the people? They're giants! We look like grasshoppers beside them!" Despite the courageous protestations of Caleb and Joshua, the people were demoralized by the report of the majority. Weeping and grumbling ensued. A woe-is-me attitude oozed through the camp. Soon, the people were ready to ditch Moses, vote in a new leader, and head back to Egypt with their tail between their legs.

Now, on one level, we can sympathize with their fear. They're just human, after all, like we are. They were stepping into the ring with Goliath-like foes. Since some of these peoples had chariots, the Israelites were out-gunned. However, they had a really good thing going for them; and that good thing was this: God. God, who had whipped every adversary in Egypt for them. God, who had given his word that they would conquer the land. God, who proved that he was the Lord of miracles. If the whole world is against you but God is on your side, your victory is assured. But, no, the Israelites chose unbelief over faith, rebellion over courage, Egyptian slavery over God-given liberation.

So, the Lord did what he is wont to do: he punished them by giving them exactly what they wanted.

People: We don't want to enter the promised land!
God: Ok, then, you will not. I'll give you what you want.

But they also got what they did not want: forty years of bearing their guilt in the wilderness, one year for every day the spies were in the land. Thus, Israel was not in the fertile land of promise but in the howling desert of waiting and wandering, until every adult who had been twenty years old at the time of the rebellion was dead and gone. Joshua and Caleb were the only two adults who made it all the way from Egypt, through the forty years, and into the promised land.

What transpired during those four decades? Considering the time span, we know relatively little. Certainly a lot of funerals, including, toward the end of the forty years, the deaths of Miriam and Aaron. More teaching about sacrifices and other elements of daily life. A rebellion by a man named Korah and his cronies over who was "in charge." Some wars and skirmishes with tribes and peoples through whose territories Israel passed. Three of the more significant occurrences involved snakes, a non-Israelite prophet, and Moses' anger.

Let's begin with the last one. The Lord told Moses that he would not be leading the Israelites into the land. Why? In what appears to have been a fit of anger at the rebellious people, Moses too rebelled. He struck the "water rock" twice, instead of speaking to it, as the Lord had told him to do. God therefore said, "Because you did not believe in me, to uphold me as holy in the eyes of the people of Israel, therefore you shall not bring this assembly into the land that I have given them" (Num. 20:12).

In the bigger picture of the salvation story, this was perfectly fitting. Moses was like the embodiment of the Law itself. He received it, relayed it, taught it, explained it, enforced it. He hefted the very tablets of stone upon which the Ten Commandments were inscribed. Now if he, Mr. Law, broke that same law, acted in unfaith, and rebelled, what chance does anyone have of keeping the law? Zilch. None. Just like Moses would die outside the promised land, so the law will not and cannot get us there. As we shall see, that job is left to the one who replaced Moses, Joshua, whose name in Greek is the same as Jesus himself. Not Moses (=the law) but Joshua (=Jesus) gets us into the promised land of salvation.

Also during these years, the Moabites tried the Rent-a-Prophet approach. They hired a seer named Balaam, a name we know from archaeological finds. He was to curse Israel, but the plan blew up in the face of the Moabites. Not only did Balaam pronounce blessings upon Israel in a series of oracles, the Lord used this non-Israelite prophet to foretell the coming of Christ. He spoke of "a star [that] shall come out of Jacob" (Num. 24:17), a title that was understood in the first century AD as a prophecy of the Messiah. In fact, the NT refers to Jesus as "the bright morning star" (Rev. 22:16), and a star acted like an ancient GPS to guide the wise men to Bethlehem, where Jesus was born (Matt. 2:1-2).

During these forty years, during yet another rebellious, grumbling period, the Lord also sent some fiery serpents into the Israelite camp. (By the way, you will often see God use animals in the Old Testament as his chosen instruments, to bring his people to their senses. Here, he uses serpents; on other occasions, he will employ a large fish, lions, bears, and locusts.) When a large number of people were bit and began to die, they begged Moses to intercede on their behalf. He did. The result? The Lord instructed Moses to make a replica of the snakes, mount it on a pole, and have the people gaze at it. When they did, they would live. So, Moses made a serpent of bronze and lifted it high, for all to see.

Ironically, the image of the problem (serpents) became the solution (life).

During a conversation that Jesus had with a Jewish religious leader named Nicodemus, he said, "As Moses lifted up the serpent in the wilderness, so must the Son of Man be lifted up, that whoever believes in him may have eternal life" (John 3:14). Being "lifted up" was Jesus' way of referring to his upcoming crucifixion. Just as the bronze serpent, imaging the problem, became the solution, so also Jesus, taking upon himself our problem of sin and death, upon the cross, became the solution as well, for in him we have forgiveness and life. For this reason, Martin Luther once called Jesus the "serpent of salvation." He became our sin so that, in a wondrous exchange, we might receive his life, healing, and righteousness.

Near the very end of the forty years, Moses delivered a two-and-a-half-hour sermon called Deuteronomy, the fifth book of the Bible and the final book of the Torah. This was his swan song, in which he repeated former teachings, rehearsed Israel's history, and exhorted them to be faithful in the future. Deuteronomy also records Moses' death and odd burial. In his one-hundred-twentieth year, he died, having seen the holy land at a distance, from atop a mountain called Pisgah. No one knows where he is buried, however, because the Lord laid his body to rest. How and under what circumstances, we are not informed. He had done his job. He had brought his people to the brink of the promised land. And there his duty ended. His protégé and long-time servant, Joshua, would take over the leadership of God's people (we will hitch a ride with him in the next chapter).

So the Torah ends. We have hitchhiked our way from creation, through the flood with Noah, through the rough and tumble lives of the patriarchs, down into Egypt, out of Egypt, and all the way to the east side of the Jordan River. These first five books, this Teaching (for that is what Torah means), will serve as the biblical bedrock for all that is to come.

The salvation story is only just beginning, but in a way, we can already see its end in sight. We have been introduced to the God who creates all things for his people, who rescues them when they are enslaved, forgives them when they rebel, provides sacrifices so they can be cleansed, dwells in the midst of the tabernacle, and has brought them to a land that will be a holy kingdom. All of this, Jesus, the Son of God, will bring to completion and perfection in himself. In him, we are recreated to be the children of God. He rescues us from the slavery to evil in which we are born. He provides unlimited forgiveness to us in his cross and resurrection. His crucifixion sacrifice gives us the atonement we desperately need. His body is our sanctuary, tabernacle, and temple. And he brings us, by baptism, into his kingdom.

In short, Jesus is the "Yes!" to all of God's promises. On every page of the Torah—indeed, every page of the Old Testament—we can write, "In many and various ways, this is about our Lord Jesus Christ and his salvation story on our behalf."

Chapter 9

Ritual Warfare in the New and National Garden of Eden

It would be nice to stick out our thumbs to a tank or armored vehicle to cruise through this chapter. Deep in the heart of a militarized zone is where we find ourselves. Battles, skirmishes, and wholesale destructions await us. Our guide is Joshua, with whom we shook hands in the last chapter. He will drive us across the dried-up Jordan, around and around the city of Jericho, and onto several battlefields. So let's climb on in and buckle up. We're about to learn about ritual warfare, land distribution, and how God deals with sin, not in fractions but in wholes.

Step inside a library, and you'll spot sections labeled Adult Books, Teen Fiction, Reference, Magazines, and so forth. The Bible is a kind of "library," a collection of sixty-six books under one roof. It too has its major sections. We just finished the first of these: the Torah ("teaching") or Pentateuch ("five books"). The next section is called by different names. English Bibles usually refer to it as the Historical Books. The twelve books in this section are Joshua, Judges, Ruth, 1-2 Samuel, 1-2 Kings, 1-2 Chronicles, Ezra, Nehemiah, and Esther. In the Hebrew Bible, however, this section is called the *Nevi'im*, which means "Prophets." Not only does it include many of those historical books, but also books named after prophets, like Isaiah, Jeremiah, etc.

That books like Joshua, Judges, Samuel, and Kings, all of which record *historical* events, are nevertheless listed among the *Prophets*, is a point worth stressing before we pick up our narrative again. The Bible never pretends to document unbiased history, sticking to empirically verifiable data. It's a different kind of history; it's prophetic, sacred, God-driven historical writing. This does not mean it's untrue or mythical. What it does mean is that, first of all, this history is co-authored by a human writer *and the Spirit*. When Christians call the Bible "inspired," that's what they mean. These writings are "God-breathed" (2 Tim. 3:16). Second, this history looks at things with a prophetic eye, that is, it sees that biblical history is marching steadily toward a goal. That goal, as we noted in the Introduction, is to get us home with the Father in Christ. That is the destination of our Lord's salvation story. So, as we read through this prophetic history, we will spot the ongoing ways that our Father is directing events, as well as dropping telltale signs of what is to come in his Son, the Messiah.

Now, to the man Joshua. In the last chapter, we left God holding the shovel beside the unmarked grave of Moses. Joshua is, in some ways, like Moses. He is the divinely appointed leader of Israel, who guides and teaches them. But unlike his predecessor, Joshua actually gets the people into the promised land, to this inheritance from the Lord. What's more, Joshua is not a prophet—at least not in the traditional sense—whereas Moses was the prophetic ideal. As I mentioned before, in Greek, the name Joshua is *Iēsous* (pronounced Yay-sous), which we write as "Jesus." Joshua as an "Old Testament Jesus" brings the people safely into the land of promise. As such, he is a type or foreshadowing of our Lord, who brings us into his Father's kingdom.

Just like some American states and modern countries have borders marked by rivers, so also in the ancient world, the boundaries of land were frequently demarcated by rivers, seas, and mountain ranges. Israel's eastern border was the Jordan River. But the Jordan also served as a kind of liminal zone, that in-between space where one transitions from "this" to "that," from "what was" to "what will be." For the people of God, the "what was" space was the wilderness, in which they had been waiting and wandering for four decades. Under Joshua, they were transitioning to "what will be." And that transitional marker was the Jordan. By the way, in the New Testament, this is why John the Baptist baptized people in the Jordan River. He was bringing them from the "what was" of waiting for the Messiah to the "what will be" of his arrival.

When it came time to make that move from "this" to "that," the Lord made it highly memorable by working a kind of historical rhyme. History didn't repeat itself, but it "rhymed" in this way: just like Israel, upon leaving Egypt, crossed the Red Sea on dry ground, so when it came time to leave the wilderness, they crossed the Jordan on dry ground. God parted the waters. His people passed over into the land which they had been promised. Along with this new beginning were other elements of renewal: they celebrated the Passover and circumcised the boys who had not yet received that mark of the covenant. Now they were ready—ready, finally—to inherit the land.

But this land was far from unoccupied. The same fierce—and, in some cases, giant—people were still dwelling there, the very people whom their parents and grandparents had cowed before. Bible teachers often jokingly refer to them as the "-ites": the Canaanites, Perizzites, Jebusites, Girgashites, and other people groups. Centuries before, the Lord summarized them under the heading of Amorites when he told Abraham that their iniquity "is not yet complete" (Gen. 15:16). He meant that, despite their ongoing, recalcitrant rebellion against him via immorality and idolatry, he would not be quick to drop the hammer. He was giving them time to amend their ways and turn to him. But they persisted in their spiritual devolution. Now the time of judgment was ripe. And the means by which the Lord would mete out that punishment would be the Israelites.

This is a crucial truth, so don't miss it. All the battles and land acquisitions in the book of Joshua were not, for instance, the ancient parallel to the move westward in the United States in the 1800s, when the lands and property of Native Americans were seized during frontier expansion. Rather, these were God's battles, God's war, in which he, as the Judge of the whole earth, was sentencing the "-ites" to destruction, then transferring their land, cities, and houses to his people. No caprice was involved. No land-hungry, bloodthirsty, basely human motivations. Instead, this was a large-scale, divinely mandated expulsion of unrepentant people from land that the Lord had declared holy.

All of this helps to explain why, for instance, the first major city to be conquered, Jericho, was destroyed in such an odd, ritualistic way. Two Israelite spies had already scoped out the place, helped in their efforts by a prostitute within the city named Rahab, who hid the men and helped them to escape. To capture Jericho, the Israelites didn't launch a frontal attack, use ladders to mount the walls, locate a secret tunnel into the city, or lay siege to it (all ways that ancient cities were taken). Instead, they marched around the city, every day, for six days, carrying the ark of the covenant with them. The ark was the throne and footstool of Yahweh; its presence was the outward sign that Israel's God was king and that he was about to establish his reign. On the seventh day, they marched seven times around the city, the priests blew rams' horns (called shofars), the Israelites let out a corporate shout, and the Lord caused the walls of Jericho to collapse. Without much effort, the people of God were able to capture the city. The whole seven-day event resembles more of an elaborate ritual than typical battlefield tactics. And rightly so. It would not be the size, strength, or martial cunning of Israel that brought them victory. God would grant them success. To him alone would be the glory. This was his war against those who, for centuries, had been battling against him.

Particularly troubling to modern readers of Joshua is that, within the borders of the land, all the inhabitants were to be killed: not only male fighters, but the women, children, and animals. Why such a wholesale destruction? For one, this land was like a national Garden of Eden for the "Adams and Eves" of Israel. Just as Adam and Eve had been commanded to guard Eden—a task they failed miserably to do!—so the Israelites were to guard the land and purge it completely of all serpentine, evil forces that would seek to seduce them into a bed of lies and idolatry. (As we shall see, when Israel failed to carry out God's will, this breach led directly to woe upon woe. The Canaanites and other "-ites" they did not destroy led them into gross and often unspeakable acts, even sacrificing their own children to other gods.)

Second, the destruction of these peoples is an unforgettable picture of how God deals with sin: in totality. The Lord was not interested in ridding 95% of the land of its Canaanite population. When it comes to evil, God is an all-or-nothing deity. In a most unexpected way, therefore, the command to purge the land completely of Canaanites was a foreshadowing of the crucifixion, where God dealt once and for all, completely, with sin. Not most sin. Not almost all sin. But all sin. Jesus wasn't just whipped or beaten or thrown in jail to suffer. No, he died. He went all the way into death that sin might be taken care of *all the way* for us.

The first half of Joshua documents the battles of Israel against these various people groups. With the notable exception of the city of Ai early on, cities and armies fell to the people of God. Through various campaigns in the north, south, and central regions of the country, they were able to gain dominance, often against enemies that outgunned and outmanned them. There are hints, however, that the hot zeal of the Israelites was beginning to chill into inertia and apathy over time. We will hear more of this dour news in the next chapter.

A significant chunk of the second half of Joshua is concerned with material that, to be quite honest, will have many readers nodding off. And that's ok! Not all parts of the Bible are equally stimulating. Many of these chapters read like pages from a surveyor's book as the land is divvied up between eleven of the tribes. Some get more, some less. Two and a half of the tribes are given land that is technically outside the promised land, east of the Jordan. Which tribe is not given land? The tribe of Levi, the tribe from which the priests and their helpers come. Rather than one whole section of the land, they are given cities that are scattered throughout the sections of the other tribes. Six of these cities are set aside as "cities of refuge." If a person had slain someone, they could flee to any of these cities to seek protection (from a possible revenge killing) until their case had been tried, and guilt or innocence determined.

As Deuteronomy ended with the death of Moses, so the book of Joshua concludes with the death of this leader. A moving speech is recorded in which he rehearses much of his people's history and not so subtly reminds them of God's uncompromising stance toward worshipping other gods. There is an ominous tone to it, as if Joshua has seen his people's future written in their past. That past is splotched with episodes of spiritual infidelity, as any reader of the Torah soon realizes. And, as we shall see directly, Joshua's message, while greatly needed, was also gravely ignored.

In this episode of the Father's ongoing salvation story, his people finally have what Abraham, Isaac, and Jacob only dreamed of having: a place to sink roots, ditch their tents and build homes, plant crops, and raise families. Most importantly, they can teach and preach and worship the God who has given all these good gifts to them, and who will do even more in time to come. Fathers can teach their sons and daughters about the rebellion of Adam and Eve, along with the Lord's promise to send the Seed who will crush the skull of the enemy. Mothers can teach their children about the time in Egypt, the crossing of the Red Sea, the hard years in the wilderness, and God's gracious gift of land to them under Joshua. Levites can instruct people in the wisdom of the Torah. Priests can serve at the tabernacle, pray, celebrate the feasts. In this new Eden, this holy land, human lives can flourish where truth and beauty and holiness are found, as the Israelites keep waiting for the Messiah to come.

All of these things "can" happen. But will they? We shall see as we bid adieu to Joshua and hitch a ride with our next guide, who will steer us into a biblical book that should be rated R for violence. Into the book of Judges we go.

Chapter 10

Everyone Did What Was Right in His Own Eyes

Have you ever driven through a crime-ridden part of a city, at night, and made sure your doors were locked? Cruising through the midnight streets of Judges is like that. You will witness anarchy, people burned to death, gang rape, mutilation, kidnapping, and more evidence of humanity's inhumanity. Obviously, these were not happy days in Israel. But there are brief, bright moments where God's love shines through in rescuers and redeemers whose deeds foreshadow Jesus, our Rescuer and Redeemer. So climb on in. Let's let men like Gideon and Samson, and a woman named Ruth, drive us through the Wild West world of Judges.

"There's always two sides to a story." Generally speaking, that adage is correct. This need not mean that the two sides are contradictory, just that there are differing perspectives on the same event. For instance, when you read the four Gospels—Matthew, Mark, Luke, and John—the first three of these often tell the same stories about Jesus, but with slightly different accents and details. Matthew is not "right" and Mark and Luke "wrong," or vice versa. Rather, they're simply telling "two [or three] sides" of the same story.

Joshua and the beginning of Judges are like that; they tell two sides of the same story about the conquest of the land. By and large, when we read Joshua, we come away with the impression that the Israelites just steamrolled over all their opponents, won all these battles, captured all these cities, and soon made Israel a Canaanite-free zone. I say "by and large" because, as I noted in the last chapter, there is evidence of Israel's creeping inertia and inability to defeat all their foes. But this is not strongly accented in Joshua. Turn to the opening chapter of Judges, however, and it's right in your face. We read of how the Israelites were unable or unwilling to drive out some of their enemies, made slaves of others, or simply lived side-by-side with these various groups of (what are often collectively called) Canaanites.

"So what?" someone might ask. "Live and let live. Coexist." That modern conception of a country being a melting pot of peoples, religions, cultures, etc., all of whom are to get along and respect one another's traditions, is not how the Lord designed ancient Israel to be. Think of it like this. Picture a huge church that covers several acres. On this campus are a sanctuary, classrooms, offices, a basketball court, parking lots, and a shed for storing tools for the groundskeepers. There is thus room within this broader space for work, worship, study, and play. However, this is still a *Christian* campus. The church will not allow a small Muslim mosque to be built in the back corner of the property, a Jewish temple in another, and several Buddhist shrines to be scattered in the sanctuary and office areas. There are clear limits to what is, and what is not, allowed on these acres precisely because they are devoted to Christianity.

So it was on the Israelite "campus," in the land that God gave to his people. The worship of Yahweh was not to exist alongside the worship of popular Canaanite deities like Baal or Asherah. The Canaanites were not even supposed to dwell on this holy soil, much less pollute it with their idolatry. As we've noted before, this land is a national Garden of Eden, where anti-Yahweh forces have no place, no rights, no mercy, not even any respect. Failure to take this seriously, God warned, would result in the adulteration of Israel's worship, the popularization of immorality, and the eventual expulsion of Israel from the same land from which they had expelled the Canaanites. Therefore, for Israel, coexistence with the Canaanites and their gods was as healthy as smoking meth while washing down rat poison with antifreeze.

But coexist they did, with disastrous consequences, some of which are described in the book of Judges. There is a cyclical nature to the narratives in Judges 1-16. Like an unfaithful spouse, the Israelites began to hook up with other gods, worshiping them instead of, or more commonly, alongside Yahweh. In the OT, idolatry is often dubbed "whoring after other gods." Other gods and goddesses were fine with their devotees "sleeping around," as it were, as long as they got some of the sacrificial action. Not Yahweh. He demands monogamous fidelity from his bride, Israel. Just as no husband would be fine with his wife being sexually faithful to him 95% of the time, so the Lord demanded nothing less than 100% fidelity from his bride.

When his people *were* unfaithful to him, God would discipline them, usually by allowing enemy nations to oppress them for a time. When the people repented and prayed to the Lord for relief, he would raise up someone to "save" or "rescue" his people (more on them in a moment). Following the military success of these leaders would be a period of rest and relative tranquility in Israel. Then, without exception, the people of God would slouch into idolatry once again. This ugly cycle of rebellion, discipline, repentance, saviors, and rest went on for centuries.

The book of Judges is named after the series of military leaders whom the Lord used to free his people from foreign oppression. But the name "Judges," in our modern context, is easily misunderstood. Picture Clint Eastwood, not Judge Judy. The Hebrew verb used to describe the actions of these "judges" is *yasha*, which means to save or deliver (the same verb is part of *Yeshua*, the Hebrew name of Jesus, our Savior). Thus, a more fitting title for the book might have been Deliverers or Saviors. *That* they rescued Israel from foreign oppression is factually true, but who they were and how they did it is much more fascinating. Let's run through a few examples.

There's Ehud. He was a southpaw who strapped a short sword to his right thigh, concealed under his cloak, and with that blade disemboweled a very fat enemy king named Eglon. This assassination led to Israel's overthrow of the Moabites. There's a fellow named Barak whom the prophetess Deborah sent to battle against a Canaanite king. Barak, no courageous hero, demurred unless Deborah agreed to join him in the ranks. She did but, in the end, the true heroine of the story was another woman named Jael, who sneakily drove a tent peg into the head of the enemy general while he was catching some Z's inside her tent. And there's Jephthah, the very definition of a rash personality, who brought victory to Israel but swore a stupid vow that ended up causing the sacrifice of his daughter (though scholars debate what this "sacrifice" actually entailed). And there are many other "judges" about whom we know very little, such as Tola, Jair, and Shamgar, the latter of whom battled the Philistines with an ox goad.

Two of the more famous judges, Gideon and Samson, further illustrate the oddball nature of these deliverers and the way they achieved success on the battlefield. Gideon is Mr. Self-Doubt. The Lord had to coax him along with sign after sign until he finally agreed to go to battle. He and his tiny army of three hundred men tiptoed under cover of night to a camp of the Midianites, shattered some clay jars, held up torches, and blasted their trumpets. In the resulting mayhem, the enemy soldiers turned on each other. Later on, Gideon's success seems to have gone to his head. He transformed spoils of war into an illicit item of worship, called an ephod, which led to idolatry in Israel.

Samson is better known for his romantic escapades with Delilah than anything else, though that dalliance was but one episode in his years of both skirt-chasing and Philistine-killing. He was what the Bible calls a Nazirite. Normally, a person was a Nazirite only for a short period, during which there were three Big No's: no barbers, no booze, no dead bodies. That is, they couldn't get a haircut, consume alcohol or any grape products, or touch anything dead. Samson, however, was a lifelong

Nazirite. He also broke his vows about as often as he kept them.

The Lord endowed Samson with supernatural strength—strength that was located on top of Samson's head, in his hair, not in his biceps, pecs, and quads. When he was tricked by his lover, Delilah, into spilling the beans about the source of his power, she had his hair cut off while he slept. With his hair gone, his strength too was scissored away. His antagonists, the Philistines, captured him, gouged out his eyes, stuck him in chains, and tried to make him the butt of their jokes during a temple festival. Samson, whose hair had begun to grow back by this time, seized the day. He prayed to the Lord to restore his strength once more. God did. Samson broke down the pillars of the temple, bringing the house down (quite literally) on everyone in attendance. He had the last laugh. We're told that this one-man-army killed more of the foes in his death than he had during his lifetime.

Samson, strong and weak, warrior and womanizer, was a splendid model of the times in which he lived. He was God's man, as the Israelites were God's people. He was unfaithful, as his people were. He made war with the Philistines, *and* he made love to them. The Lord used him, but he also misused his position for ungodly activity. All too often, Samson did what was right in his own eyes. That worldview, that twisted "moral" compass, is repeated in Judges: "In those days there was no king in Israel. Everyone did what was right in his own eyes" (17:6; 21:25). Those are the closing and climactic lines of the book, uttered after five chapters of harrowing incidents involving idolatry, rape, butchering of corpses, and other scenes of carnage and anarchy.

Everyone did what was right in his own eyes. If there's even been a guaranteed way to create hell on earth, that's it.

As bad as things were in Judges, however, there were telltale signs of hope and renewal, like little blades of green grass growing through the cracks of a hard and lifeless sidewalk. The most important of these is preserved in the beautiful little book called Ruth, which immediately follows Judges and is set within that time period. Here is the story of a family that has lost about everything. Father? Dead. Two sons? Dead. The only ones left were the mom, Naomi, and her two daughters-in-law, one of whom pledged to stay with her, come what may. That daughter-in-law, Ruth, was not an Israelite but a woman from Moab, one of the countries neighboring Israel to the east. The book named after Ruth tells the story of her selfless devotion to Naomi, the women's struggles in the town of Bethlehem, and Ruth's eventual marriage to a man named Boaz, who served as a redeemer for the family.

Boaz and Ruth were the great-grandparents of David, the boy from Bethlehem who would grow up to be the greatest king Israel ever had, as well as the king whose regal office foreshadowed Jesus, who is frequently called the Son of David. We will learn much more about David in Chapters 12-13. The book of Ruth, with its themes of renewal, redemption, and hope for a better future reminds us that, despite the best efforts of humanity to ruin life in this world, this world is still *God's* world, not ours. And he was steering events, great and small, toward the goal of history in the birth of his Son to redeem humanity.

As you read through Judges, with its dark humor, sexcapades, and violence, one obvious but shocking truth to keep remembering is this: these are God's people. The Israelites were what we today call "the church," the body of believers. Were they a good church? Obviously not! Here was a mass of sinners, making a mess of things, doing what was right in their own eyes, often acting in morally atrocious ways. But the Lord was stubbornly committed to his promises to them, even as he is to us, despite all the ugliness that often bedevils the church (and individual believers) still today. His mercy, not our sin, will always speak louder.

Okay, you might need a little breather after this chapter. I understand! Hitchhiking through some of these stories is not for the faint of heart. What's on the horizon? We're about to meet one of Israel's greatest prophets, Samuel, as well as the country's first king, a tall fellow named Saul. Changes are coming. Changes in leadership, unity, and much more. Onward we go, steadily working our way home.

Chapter 11

Saul "The Rock": Mule Hunter, King #1, and Madman

As you drive across America, you'll see the landscape change from coastal areas to mountains, plains, deserts, and more. The biblical landscape undergoes its own alter-ations. We'll see firsthand a major shift in our ride through this chapter. Patriarchs have transported us. Prophets and priests have given us a lift. But now, for the first time, the man behind the wheel wears a crown. And this king, Israel's first in a long line, has the seat pulled way back to make room for those long legs. Tall Saul is our driver, along with the prophet who put him into office, Samuel. These two will take us into the story of bad priests, a stolen ark, kingship, disobedience, and even a noctur-nal visit to a witch. Welcome to 1 Samuel.

When I drove a truck in the old field, I worked with a guy who, quite literally, wore his political convictions on his sleeve. His tattoo read "Anarchist." He's the only one of those I've ever known. I think it's safe to say that most of us agree, however begrudgingly, that some form of government is necessary. In ancient times, most leadership was centered in a clan chief, monarch, or group of elders. The seeds of democracy sprouted in ancient Greece and, of course, are in full flower today. Socialism, communism, and other forms of government have also arisen in our world. Some of these political systems are better, some worse, and a few are godawful. None, however, are perfect. Why? Every governing and voting group is composed of sinners, who are always going to make a mess of things. Indeed, a "political mess" seems a redundant phrase to most of us.

What kind of governance do we see in the Old Testament? Who led God's people? Up to this point in our story, the primary ruling authorities were elders. This group is referred to several times in the Torah as a distinct set of men who assisted Moses and Joshua as well as resolved disputes. Cities and villages had their own elders, too, who addressed local issues and made rulings in an area of town known as the "gate." The gate was the city entrance but also the public area where questions were debated and decisions handed down. There was certainly no democracy in Israel, but neither was there a monarchy. Not yet anyway. Even though Moses and Joshua, along with some of the judges, exercised a king-like leadership, none of them were given or used that title. A first-century Jewish historian named Flavius Josephus coined the word "theocracy" to describe Israel's governance; it means "ruled by God." Israel's only king was Yahweh. But, as we shall see shortly, that was about to change.

To explain how this change came about, we first need to get acquainted with the second major prophet in the Bible, a fellow named Samuel. We shake hands with him in the opening chapters of the twin set of books named after him, 1 and 2 Samuel. These books might have been more fittingly named 1 and 2 David, since he soon emerges as the dominant character.

The boy Samuel really had two families: the biological family into which he was born, and the priestly family in which he grew up. Both were a bit of a wreck. His dad was a polygamist, with two wives. One of them was named Peninnah; she sounds as sweet as Cruella de Vil. The other was Hannah, Samuel's mom. Before Samuel was born, she had struggled for years with infertility. Finally, in answer to her prayers, God opened her womb and baby Samuel made his entrance into the world. The Hebrew name of this little answer to prayer is Shmuel, which quite fittingly means "heard by God."

Remember how in the last chapter we talked about the "no haircut" Nazirites, of whom Samson was one? Samuel was too. Hannah vowed to God that, should he give her a child, she would devote her child to the Lord as a Nazirite. This she did. When Samuel was just a preschooler, his mother brought him to live and grow up at the tabernacle in Shiloh, under the tutelage of an old priest named Eli. Hannah's part in the story concludes with a beautiful song, sung by this mother. It's the Old Testament parallel to the song sung by another mother, the Virgin Mary, in the New Testament. You can read Hannah's in 1 Samuel 2 and Mary's in Luke 1.

What was this priestly family like with which Samuel grew up? Imagine a church where the senior pastor is a gray-haired, overweight, apathetic father and his two good-for-nothing sons are the associate pastors. While the brothers are having sex with numerous female church workers and skimming cash from the offering plate, the old man turns a blind eye to their evil ways or offers only a half-hearted rebuke. That's Eli and his sons. That's the priestly family in which Samuel grew from a tiny tot into a man. In fact, the first sermon that the Lord gives young Samuel to preach is that disaster will befall his adopted priestly family. And it does. When the Israelites go out to battle against the Philistines, both the sons of Eli are killed, and the ark of the covenant is taken as the spoils of war. Their father, when he hears the news, falls over backward in his chair, breaks his neck, and dies on the spot. A sad end to a bad situation.

As God is prone to do, however, from the wreckage of this death and defeat, he constructed a new hope for his people. He built Samuel; he built him up to be a prophet, judge, and leader. And a good one he was, but... (there's always a "but," right?) Samuel seems to have suffered from the same problem many of us still face today: he repeated the mistakes of his own upbringing. He was raised by a priest who had also raised two rebellious sons. And it sounds like Samuel's own sons didn't turn out much better than Eli's two sons. Rather than following the faithful way of their father, they took bribes and perverted justice. Things got so bad that the Israelites bellyached to Samuel about his sons' wicked ways. But that wasn't all. They wanted to fill up this gap in faithful leadership with something that other nations had, but which was radically novel for Israel: a king.

The real beef that God had with Israel for asking for a king was not the office per se. Already, back in Moses' day, he had spoken of a future king and laid down Do's and Don'ts for the ruler (Deut. 17:14-20). The problem was this: they wanted to be like all the other nations. Remember, "all the other nations" are the very ones that Israel was to be *un*like. Aping the Canaanites and other "ites" was never a good move for the Lord's people: "Hey, let's imitate those people…you know, *the ones that God devoted to destruction because of their evil.*" So, to paraphrase what the Lord said to Samuel: "Listen, they're rejecting me as their true king, not you. This is one more act of rebellion on their mile-long rap sheet. They want a king? Fine. Give them what they want; *that will be their punishment.* Only make sure they know beforehand that the three favorite verbs of this king will be 'take, take, take.' Take their children to be his servants and soldiers. Take their money through taxation. Take their land and crops for his own." Samuel relayed this dire prediction to the people, but his words fell on deaf ears. They were dead set on sticking the crown on somebody's head. And, in no time at all, they did.

If the NBA had been around back then, one of the starters on the Israelite team might have been a guy named Saul. The Bible is famously reticent about the physical descriptions of people, but not Saul. We are told that he was "a handsome young man. There was not a man among the people of Israel more handsome than he. From his shoulders upward he was taller than any of the people" (1 Sam. 9:2). Good looks. Superior height. Sounds like the Old Testament's Dwayne "The Rock" Johnson, as my cohost, Daniel Emery Price, nick-named him on our podcast, "40 Minutes in the Old Testament." Saul "The Rock."

We meet Saul when he's just a man roaming the hillsides of Judea, on the hunt for his father's lost donkeys. When he comes back home, a few days later, he has been "changed into another man," as the Bible puts it (1 Sam. 10:6). Samuel finds him and anoints him. He's filled with the Spirit and prophesies. He's publicly acclaimed king by Israel. Talk about a dizzying turn of events for this young man! From donkey hunter to head of a nation in a matter of days.

Not long afterward, Saul the Rock is given the chance to show his fellow citizens he's got what it takes to lead the nation. An Israelite city called Jabesh-gilead is besieged by the enemy and given a horrific ultimatum: die or surrender but have your right eye gouged out. Needless to say, neither are appealing alternatives. When Saul is informed, he leaps into action. He rallies the troops, attacks the next day, and the would-be eye-gougers are sent running for the hills. Not only did this victory demonstrate Saul's military prowess, it also gave him the chance to be magnanimous to some of his fellow citizens who earlier had scoffed at his abilities. A win-win situation. The people rejoiced. Worship happened. A sort of second acclamation of his kingship took place. As Charles Dickens might say, there were "great expectations" for this newbie king.

Saul's sweet beginning, however, soon soured. Centuries before, shortly after Israel had exited Egypt, a group called the Amalekites had cowardly and mercilessly attacked them from the rear, picking off the weak and weary stragglers. Back then, God had told Moses that eventually he wanted the very memory of the Amalekites to be wiped out. Under Saul, that time of judgment finally came. The king and his army went to battle and won a decisive victory against the Amalekites. Rather than destroying them all, however, Saul spared the king and the choicest of the livestock. When Samuel confronted him for his disobedience, Saul waffled, blame-shifting and claiming it was the people's idea to spare the enemy. Samuel was both heartbroken and furious. He knew what this meant. A king who would not follow the word of God was not fit to be the king of God's people. The prophet leveled this hard but clear word at the king: the Lord will tear the kingdom away from you and give the throne to someone else. Who that "someone else" was is left unmentioned. But in no time at all, as the story unfolds, we learn that Saul's replacement will be a young shepherd, a teenager, who lived in Bethlehem. His name was David.

After Saul's disobedience and Samuel's rebuke, the king's life begins to spin out of control. We read that an "evil spirit" terrorized him. Today we'd say he had a mental breakdown. He was phobic about everything. He thought everyone was against him. Things got so bad that he started throwing spears at his servants and even his son, Jonathan. As we will hear more about in the next chapter, Saul became fixated on hunting down David, using all his resources and energy to take out his rival.

Right before his battlefield death, Saul finally hit rock bottom. God wouldn't talk to him anymore. Samuel, by this point, had died of old age. Saul was still a believer in the Lord, but he could no longer get any guidance from dreams or prophets. In his desperation, he made a stupid and wicked decision: he disguised himself to visit a witch, a necromancer, to ask her to call up Samuel from the grave so that he could consult the prophet as to what he should do. In one of the Bible's strangest and spookiest scenes, Samuel comes up out of the earth but is none too pleased to have been disturbed.

Just as blunt in his afterlife as he was in this life, the prophet harangues Saul for his disobedience, repeats the warning that God will hand over the kingship to another (he actually names David this time), and finally tells Saul that he will die in battle the next day—he and his sons. That is how the book of 1 Samuel ends, with this prophecy coming true. Saul is wounded in battle and falls on his own sword. Three of his sons are also killed in action. The only bit of good news salvaged from this depressing end is that Samuel had told Saul that, when he died, the king would be "with me." Whatever Saul's faults may have been—and they were many—he and his sons did join the Lord's prophet in the afterlife.

Perhaps you're thinking: Wow, Israel's first king did not bode well for the future of royalty among the Lord's people! You'd be half right and half wrong. Half right in that, yes, the overwhelming majority of kings in Israel would be rotten, selfish, fickle leaders, more given to bowing before idols than clinging faithfully to God. As I mentioned earlier, the Israelites' punishment was getting the very kings they craved.

But there's also the half-wrong side. The kings in Israel, especially David and the David-like leaders whom we will hear about in the coming chapters, occupied an important office in the Old Testament. As kings, they foreshadowed the King of kings, the Messiah Jesus. Though none of them ruled perfectly over the kingdom of God, they did point forward to the King who would. In the Gospels, Jesus is called the "Son of David" and "King." He came to proclaim and usher in the "kingdom of God," that is, the active reign of the Lord on earth through his Son. On the cross, where the sign read, "Jesus of Nazareth, the King of the Jews," we see the truth proclaimed. The cross is also his throne. He reigns there, exercising his power in mercy, his royalty in speaking forgiveness. He came to reign by serving, by giving his life for us all.

We have heard, a few times now, about this teenager named David. It's now time to find out more. So say adios to Samuel and Saul. And let's head a few miles south of Jerusalem to the little town of Bethlehem, to meet this famous son of Jesse.

Chapter 12

He of Whom All the Girls Sang

Even those who have never read a page of the Bible know that a "David vs. Goliath" situation pits an underdog against an overwhelming force. But who is this "David" character anyway? We will find out as we drive through this chapter and the next. We'll see him rise from shepherd to warrior to king. But the man in the driver's seat is not just another hero; he's the man who, long after, will be remembered as the one who left an indelible imprint upon the minds of Israelites. If a pollster had asked the average Jew on the streets of first-century Jerusalem which Old Testament character the Messiah would be like, most would answer, "David, of course."

Have you ever been around someone whom God seems to have spent a little extra time on? I mean they have check marks by all the boxes. Good looks? Yes. Athletic? Yes. Musically talented? Yes. Precocious courage, confidence, and intelligence? Yes. And, as if all these gifts were not enough, they are good leaders, likable, and always seem to get their own way with people. Take all those qualities, and add to them some acting skills, street smarts, and a way with the ladies, and you have the portrait of the young man David.

A solid argument can be made that, besides Moses, David is the most impactful person in the Old Testament story of salvation. Jerusalem, one of the most important cities in world history, became important only because David captured it to make it the capital city of Israel. He is the paradigmatic king of Israel, against whom all other kings are compared or contrasted. The Psalms are incredibly influential on the worship and beliefs of God's people; almost half of them were written by David. The Lord promised him that one of his descendants would be the Messiah and sit on his throne. Indeed, so closely aligned is David with the Messiah that the Savior is even nicknamed "David" by some of the prophets.

When we consider all of this, we might suppose that David, like, say, Alexander the Great, was the son of a renowned leader, under the tutelage of famous scholars from boyhood. He was the kind of kid whom onlookers would point to and say, "See that boy? There goes the future of our nation." But no, that wasn't David at all. Gifted though he was, David was an unknown country boy, tucked away in a backwater village in the Judean hill country, the youngest of eight boys fathered by a man named Jesse. His dad raised sheep, of which the teenager David was the shepherd. Presumably, his life would have been no different than the lives of tens of thousands of others in Israel whose names historians had no reason to record. But one day, the prophet Samuel showed up in his village of Bethlehem. From that moment, David's life, and our lives still today, were forever changed.

You will recall, from the last chapter, that Samuel had informed a disobedient Saul that his days as king were numbered. Saul's subsequent paranoia necessitated that Samuel be sneaky about his anointing of Saul's replacement. Directed by God, he surreptitiously journeyed to Bethlehem, met with Jesse, and had him parade all of his sons before him. One, two, three, four, five, six, seven, all of them walked before the prophet. Though some of them looked like regal material to Samuel, to each of them God shook his head. He reminded Samuel that he "looks at the heart," that is, the whole interior disposition of a person. None of them had what the Lord was looking for. Then, in a comical moment, when Samuel asks Jesse if he has any more sons, it's like the father slaps his forehead and says, "Oh, yeah, I almost forgot! There is the youngest boy, but he's out taking care of the sheep." David is fetched from the field. When he appears, the Lord says to the prophet, "Arise, anoint him, for this is he" (1 Sam. 16:12). A horn of olive oil was poured on the boy's head and the Spirit of God came upon him. David became a little "m" messiah, which in Hebrew means "anointed one."

The Lord's choice of David is a crucial lesson in his divinely backward way of doing things. In story after story, the Lord passes over the obvious candidates. He will use old, infertile women to bear promised sons, not newlywed twenty-year-olds. Frequently, it will be non-Israelites like Ruth or Rahab who exhibit a fidelity to God that outshines the Israelites. The Lord repeatedly bypasses firstborn sons to choose the younger or, as in David's case, the youngest in the family.

God does this not just to keep us on our toes, but to show us that his ways are not our ways, that he tends to hide himself beneath his opposite. This upside-down way of God finds its ultimate fulfillment in Jesus, who also is born in Bethlehem, who is raised in the rural village of Nazareth, who looked no different outwardly than other people, and who was publicly executed by the Roman state in a manner purposefully designed to be shameful and horrific. Yet who is Jesus? He is God in the flesh, the extraordinary concealed in the ordinary, even in the shame and seeming foolishness of the cross.

The rest of David's life is worthy of a three-hour cinematic experience. We will focus on a few scenes from 1 Samuel that paint a portrait of this man.

This first part could be called David's young and wild years, full of battles and near-misses and his early romances with a growing harem of wives. As a teenager, he boldly agrees to a one-on-one match with an extraordinarily large soldier from Philistia named Goliath. David takes him down with a stone shot from his sling, a deadly ancient battlefield weapon, then chops off his head with Goliath's massive sword.

If you've read Homer's *Iliad*, you know that the soldiers frequently made speeches on the battlefield as they prepared to exchange blows. David makes his own before killing Goliath. He drives home the point that this is not his battle; it's God's battle. He will not be victorious because he's the better soldier but because he comes in the name of the Lord. When you read the Psalms of David, you hear echoes of this same language. This young soldier, unarmored and armed only with a sling, may appear to be the underdog, but don't be deceived. He is most certainly not. If God is on your side and a whole world of giants is against you, they are the underdog, not you. David is victorious, in other words, because the Lord fought in and through him. It is no different when Jesus, the Son of David, takes on the giants of sin and death on the battlefield of the cross and resurrection. Christ's victory for us was never in doubt because the Father's commitment to Jesus was never in doubt. He came in the name of the Lord to fight and win for us.

David's giant-slaying was the moment he experienced the ancient version of "going viral." Gone were the days of his anonymity. He and Saul's son, Jonathan, linked up as the closest of friends. So obvious were David's military skills that the king appointed him general of his army. When he and his troops returned from battle, women would serenade them with songs about David. Such adulation, however, proved to be a double-edged sword, for the very songs that praised David did so by comparing him to Saul—comparisons in which David always came out on top. This rise in young David's popularity also gave rise to fear, dread, and jealousy in an increasingly belligerent Saul.

First by stealth and then openly, Saul made it his mission to exterminate this young upstart who had a whole nation swooning over him. In an attempt to kill David by the hands of the enemy, the king promised him his daughter, Michal, in marriage, but only if he paid a bridal dowry of one hundred Philistine foreskins (surely the weirdest dowry ever!). Never one to back down from a challenge, David returned with *two hundred* foreskins and became the king's son-in-law. When Saul's bodyguard failed to murder David, the king tried to skewer him with a spear. When David fled to the hills and gathered around him a band of fiercely loyal fighters, Saul initiated a nationwide manhunt. On more than one occasion, wily David snuck so close to Saul that he could easily have put a blade to his throat, but he would not lay a hand on the Lord's anointed. Later, in an ironic twist, David, top menace to the Philistines, was actually welcomed into the enemy camp as he was eluding Saul. Not until the battlefield death of the king, which we discussed in the previous chapter, was David finally safe to return to his land and people.

At the very center of the Bible, literally and figuratively, is the book of Psalms. These 150 poems, about half of which are authored by David, range from hymns of praise to laments to reflections on the Word of God and the history of Israel. The psalms are uniquely words from God that become our prayerful words back to God. Quotes from them or echoes of them are woven through the life of Jesus, from his conception to his crucifixion. As you read them—or better yet, pray them—keep in mind that these 150 poems are a digest of all that the Scriptures teach us about God, ourselves, and the salvation work of the Messiah.

We might assume that this turning point in David's life was when things would finally start to fall in place for him. And, in one sense, we would be right. David would be crowned king of a portion of Israel, then, after a few years, consolidate his power over the entire nation. He would capture Jerusalem and establish it as his capital. He would reduce surrounding peoples to vassal status and be promised that the Messiah would be his descendant. So, yes, David's sun was certainly beginning to rise just as Saul's sun set.

On the other hand, the God of David, the same God who is still at work in our lives today, is often a nocturnal deity. Not at the noon of success but at the midnight of trial, he arises to enter our hearts and begin the defining labor of unmaking and remaking us into the children he wants us to be. It is no coincidence that many of the beautiful psalms by David were written during these ugly years. He cries out in anguish of soul from a cave. He laments what he feels is the Lord's absence in a barren wasteland. Though David certainly did not want or welcome this season of suffering, the fruit that it bore in his life is ample testimony that God was anything but absent from him. He was there in the thick of his pain. The dark wilderness was the Lord's workshop for building David into the man and the king whom he would one day become.

More than anything else, God was showing David that he was the only God David needed. The Philistines had their deity. The Ammonites and Moabites had theirs. David's world, as much as our own, had no shortage of god options on the religious menu. But all these other so-called deities offered their devotees the same thing that money or sex or power offers their worshippers today: a mouthful of salt when dying of thirst. Rather than satisfying their adherents, false gods only amplify the need. They cannot love. They cannot forgive. What they can, and repeatedly do, do is dehumanize their worshipers. Those who bow at their altars are themselves altered into people with beastly souls who act utterly contrary to the way the Creator has made them to be. For this reason, David often uses animal metaphors in the psalms to depict those who war against the true God. They are like dogs, roaming the streets of the city. They are like lions, eager to tear and devour their prey. They are like serpents, whose poison is on their slandering tongues. Idolatry produces a human zoo pretending to be a temple.

In these early years of David's life, from his secret anointing in Bethlehem to the public proclamation of him as king after the death of Saul, the Lord was making David keenly aware that his only hope, his only salvation, was in him. For that reason, David's life was a template for the life of the Son of David. Both were born in the same town. Both had to go into exile to escape murder by kings (Saul and Herod). Both were plotted against, slandered, and eventually reigned in Jerusalem: David from his throne and Jesus from his cross. The Son of David knew that his Father was with him; he trusted him. Many times, words lifted from the psalms of David were found on the lips of Jesus. What these psalms said about David, they said with even greater accuracy about Christ.

We will need another chapter to finish up with David's life, but this part of the trip should be enough to make us fully aware that a Bible without David would be like a history of playwrights without Shakespeare or a rock 'n roll documentary without the Beatles or Rolling Stones. Most of what we talked about so far is covered in 1 Samuel. Let's turn the page now to 2 Samuel, where we will learn more about David's reign, his downfall, and a tattered family history that eventually leads to his son, Solomon, who reigns in David's place.

Chapter 13

David's Downward Spiral

We're moving uphill in this chapter, from the coastal plain beside the Mediterranean, through the foothills of Judea, and up into the mountains. Our destination? Jerusalem. In fact, once we find a good spot, we will park the vehicle for quite a while. Instead of hitchhiking, we'll stroll through the narrow streets of this holy city for a chapter or three. David has made this location his capital, as it will be for his son, Solomon, and all the kings that follow him. Here, we'll see David upend his life, Solomon reign wisely then ruin terribly, and a string of rulers come afterward, most of whom will slouch toward idolatry. We will get to that sordid history, but first we need to round out David's life, reign, and death.

With Saul out of the picture, we might think that everything was smooth sailing for David. He'd take the reins of Israel and lead them onward as king. The people would rally behind this good-looking, beloved giant slayer. But things were a bit bumpy at first. For the first seven and a half years, although David had been

anointed as king of the nation, he was more like a mere
chieftain to his own tribe of Judah.

Here's what went down: one of Saul's surviving
sons Ish-Bosheth had taken his dad's place as king
over most of the twelve tribes of Israel. The country
was divided; a civil war of sorts ensued, with ongoing
skirmishes between north and south. But when Ish-
Bosheth's general, a man named Abner, switched to
David's side, the days of Saul's son were numbered.
After he had defected to the south, however, things went
south for this turncoat. Abner was assassinated by Joab,
one of David's generals. Later, Ish-Bosheth was assassinated by two of his own compatriots. As has often happened in world history, the opening years of these kings'
reigns were disfigured by brutality and bloodshed.

That is a fact worth noting: biblical history is the
record of God's guidance of events toward their goal in
Jesus, to be sure, but these same events are besmirched by
backstabbings, sexual escapades, rebellions, and grossly
selfish acts of men and women. The story of the Bible is
not a neat and tidy documentary of upstanding citizens
who dutifully perform righteous acts to shepherd history
toward its culmination in Christ. Rather, it's the story of
sinners doing sinful things, all of which the wise Lord
of history nevertheless uses for good, for his ultimate
purpose of saving us. If God were to wait around for
perfect people to engage in holy deeds to accomplish his
merciful plan of salvation, it would never happen. Those
"perfect people" don't exist. All the Father has to work
with are sinful, weak people, just like ourselves.

Finally, after trailing David from his being a youthful shepherd to national hero to tribal chieftain, we
now see him elevated, at the age of thirty, to a powerful

monarch over a united Israel. He's a man with many
wives by this time, as well as a growing number of children. One of his first tasks was to establish a capital
city, which he does when he captures Jerusalem from its
original inhabitants, the Jebusites. Though David was
born in Bethlehem, that old part of Jerusalem would
thereafter be called "the city of David." If you visit Israel
today, you can take a tour through this part of the city.
There, ancient stone walls are still visible, where archae-
ologists have dug down to David's time (the 900s BC).

With Jerusalem under his control, David also
decided it was time to relocate his nation's holiest object
to the city: the ark of the covenant. This was the Lord's
footstool, from which he reigned between the two golden
cherubim on either side. As David, God's chosen king,
reigned in Jerusalem, so it was fitting that David's God,
the King of kings, should have this throne-emblem there
as well. Though the ark's arrival in Jerusalem was initially
delayed by an outburst of divine anger when it was incor-
rectly transported, eventually the ark was borne into the
city with joyful fanfare, with David dancing before it.

For generations, since Israel had camped at Mt.
Sinai, God had been moving about in a tent (the tabernacle) for his dwelling. About this time, with the kingdom firmly under David's control, the king decided it
was high time that a permanent structure, a temple, be
built for the Lord. But God said, "Not so fast." That
temple would be built, for sure, but it would be David's
son, Solomon, who would oversee the construction.
Instead, the Lord said, "I have a better idea." God would
build a "house" for David—not an edifice of wood or
stone but a dynasty-house. His sons and grandson and
great-grandsons would sit on the throne in Jerusalem.

Even better, much better (!), one of David's descendants would sit on this throne to reign over a kingdom that would never end.

This promise, voiced in 2 Samuel 7, is of paramount importance in the story of salvation. It stands, like a mountain, from the peak of which we can gaze into the unfolding future. Since the Lord first told Adam and Eve that a seed, a descendant, would one day arise to destroy the work of the devil by crushing his head, believers had been waiting. The promise was passed to Noah, to Abraham, to Moses, and on down the line. Gradually, the people from whom this descendant would come had narrowed—from humanity in general to Abraham's line to the tribe of Judah. When God gave David this promise, it narrowed even further—the Messiah, the long-awaited Savior, would come from his family tree. That is why, when Jesus was conceived inside the virgin womb of Mary, the angel Gabriel told her, "He will be great and will be called the Son of the Most High. And the Lord God will give to him the throne of his father David, and he will reign over the house of Jacob forever, and of his kingdom there will be no end" (Luke 1:32-33). This is also why, as the Gospels tell the story of Jesus, they record multiple occasions when people spoke of Jesus as the "Son of David." This is also why, as I noted in the previous chapter, the OT prophets sometimes referred to the Messiah as "David."

There's part of me that wishes we could wrap up this chapter on such a high and positive note. But we can't. If we did, we would neglect what the Bible does not shy away from recording: David's downfall. And not just his downfall but the many life-altering, family-destroying repercussions that arose from it. We will only highlight a few of these low points, but you can read them in vivid detail in 2 Samuel 11 to 1 Kings 2.

It all began during an evening stroll upon the flat roof of the king's palace. From his elevated position, David spied a woman bathing. A very beautiful woman. He made some inquiries to discover who she was. The story should have ended there, not only because David was already committing the sin of lust, but because he was informed that she was Bathsheba, wife of one of David's closest friends, a fellow soldier named Uriah. But sadly, the story was far from over. Bathsheba was summoned to the palace, where she and the king had sex. How willing or unwilling Bathsheba was is never mentioned in the Bible (Hebrew has a word for "rape"; it is not used here). What we do know is that only David is blamed for this sexual sin, not Bathsheba.

Not long after, Bathsheba, finding she was pregnant, informed David. Rather than confessing his sin, the king tried to cover it up. He called Uriah away from the battlefield, back to Jerusalem. David assumed this soldier would happily take advantage of his leave to spend some romantic hours with his lovely wife. That way, when Bathsheba began showing, no one would question the paternity of the child. But David's plan fell apart. A faithful and stalwart soldier, Uriah refused any comforts of home while his fellow warriors were risking their lives on the battlefield. He slept, every night, on the porch of the palace, along with the servants, even though his home was obviously within sight of the palace. Finally, frustrated with Uriah's refusal, David stooped to the lowest level yet: he sent a message to the general that said, more or less, "Get rid of Uriah and make it appear as a casualty of war." And who bore this message? Uriah himself. Unbeknownst to him, he carried his death sentence in his pocket.

Afterward, the downward spiral of David only quickened. Uriah was killed on the battlefield, along with others. The king, in a hypocritical show of "mercy," took the war widow, Bathsheba, as his own wife. A son was born to them. The prophet Nathan confronted David to call him to repent of his wickedness of murder and taking another man's wife. The king did confess and was forgiven. Nevertheless, the child born to Bathsheba became sick and died, as God decreed he would. But the death of this child, a direct result of David's sin, was only the beginning of the king's woes. Nathan told him, in no uncertain terms, that a sword now hung over David's house, and that evil would arise from the king's own family.

And evil did arise, in spades. One of David's sons Amnon lusted after and raped his half-sister, Tamar. Her full brother, Absalom, bided his time then took revenge on her attacker, his half-brother, by arranging for Amnon's murder. To escape punishment, Absalom fled the country to live with his mother's relatives. When David finally let his son return, he gave him a cold welcome, even refusing to see him for two whole years. Absalom had had enough of his father. This son of David was a strikingly handsome man, renowned for his long hair. He began to steal the hearts of fellow Israelites, glad-handing them at the gate of Jerusalem, disparaging his father as a hardhearted king from whom they could never get justice. Finally, when the iron was hot, Absalom struck. He staged a successful military coup. As his father and his supporters fled for their lives, Absalom took over. To make it 100% clear that he was now ruler, he staged a public spectacle: he set up a tent on the roof of the palace—the very place where David had been a peeping Tom—and had sex with all of his father's concubines.

The book of 2 Samuel spends several chapters on this coup, its preliminary success and eventual failure. David was able, via some advisers who were secretly working for him, to steer Absalom toward some bad military decisions which led to his eventual defeat and death. Ironically, his famous long hair cut short his life. It got caught in a tree as his mule ran underneath the limbs. He was hanging there when David's forces found him, making him a human target for the spears of Joab, David's top general, who executed him on the spot. Despite all that Absalom had done to bring havoc into David's life, this rebel was still his son. And this king, in one of the most heartbreaking laments in the Bible, cries out when he hears of Absalom's death, "O my son Absalom, my son, my son Absalom! Would I had died instead of you, O Absalom, my son, my son!" (2 Sam. 18:33).

What more shall we say of David's latter years? After his son's takeover and defeat, a man named Sheba staged another rebellion, this one easily and quickly put down. The land suffered through a three-year famine. David angered God during a census and brought a plague upon the land that killed tens of thousands of Israelites. Finally, we see David as an old man, shivering in bed, warmed by the body of a beautiful young virgin, with two of his sons vying for the throne, and David issuing revenge orders about so-and-so and so-and-so whom Solomon is to kill after David has died. It's very ugly. It's disappointing, gross even. What happened to that young shepherd boy who was the man after God's own heart?

That young shepherd boy became a man who did what men often do, especially those in positions of power. He became narcissistic. He neglected his family. Things fell apart, badly. And it was not only David that suffered. So did his family, friends, and countless citizens.

You might be wondering—quite understandably!—how in the world that David, with all these faults, became The Model King for Israel, against whom all subsequent kings were measured? It's quite simple: no matter how many times and in how many ways David jacked up his life, he always returned to the one true God for forgiveness. Unlike almost every king that followed him, David did not bow the knee to Baal or Asherah or Molech or any other idol. He knew and believed that in the Lord alone is forgiveness. In the one true God, we meet a Father who not only can but gladly does blot out our sins. No false god can do that. Idols will leave you alone with your sins, with no way to atone for them. But, as David writes in one of his many psalms, "There is forgiveness with you [O Lord]" (Ps. 130:4). And, "I acknowledged my sin to you, and I did not cover my iniquity; I said, 'I will confess my transgressions to the LORD,' and you forgave the iniquity of my sin" (32:5).

Here we are then. "The king is dead, long live the king!" But two of his sons are claiming to be the rightful heir to the throne. Which will it be? And we are still stuck in Jerusalem, walking the streets, listening to the chatter of the people, every eye cast up toward the palace. What will happen next? We'll see in the next chapter, as Bathsheba will reemerge into the story to pave the way for the coronation of her son.

Chapter 14

Solomon, the Wisest Fool

The tension is palpable in the streets of Jerusalem. Up in the palace, gray-haired David is in bed. His time is short. Not far from Jerusalem, the king's oldest living son is partying it up with his cronies, firmly convinced he will soon place his posterior on the regal throne. There are also rumors afloat of some backroom political maneuvering that would result in another son Solomon being crowned straightaway, while David is still around to give a thumbs up to that choice. What will happen? Let's tiptoe into the royal residence and eavesdrop on the conversations transpiring there. We are now entering the history recorded in 1 and 2 Kings, then retold in 1 and 2 Chronicles.

We sometimes attach adjectives to the names of famous and infamous leaders in world history. Think of Ivan the Terrible, Honest Abe, Alexander the Great, Richard the Lionheart, and so forth. Whether these nicknames are entirely accurate is up for debate (I mean, was Ivan *always* terrible or Lincoln *always* honest?). But, fully accurate or not, the names are entrenched in our cultural memory. In this chapter, we will meet another man whose name is bound to an adjective: Wise Solomon or Solomon the Wise. In his case, the description is accurate, but only halfway. This king of Israel was rich in wisdom, without a doubt, but he was also arguably the wisest *fool* who ever lived.

We'll get to both Solomon's wisdom and folly in a minute, but before we do, let's quickly deal with the court intrigue surrounding his coronation as co-regent with David.

The logical choice for the next king was Adonijah. He was David's oldest surviving son. Adonijah had no qualms about proclaiming, "I will be king," even while his dad was still above ground (1 Kings 1:5). He and his supporters staged a grand old jamboree to celebrate his soon-to-be donning of the crown. But he jumped the gun, big time. David had never told Adonijah that he would be king.

So who had David selected as his heir to the throne? Solomon.

While Adonijah was having his bash a little ways out of town, an unlikely pair of people teamed up to remind David of his earlier promise. The pair? Bathsheba (you'll remember her from the previous chapter) and Nathan (the prophet who called David to repent for murdering Bathsheba's husband). Unlikely pair, indeed. After the death of their first son, David and Bathsheba had another son, whom they named Solomon. When Nathan and Bathsheba informed David of Adonijah's snatching at the crown and already dubbing himself "king," David acted quickly to make known his will.

David decreed that Solomon should ride upon the king's royal mule, be anointed, and publicly acclaimed the new king amidst trumpet blasts and shouts from the crowds. And so it happened. The very ground quaked under the feet of those who were dancing, shouting, and making music to greet King Solomon. As you might suspect, this news threw a very wet blanket on Adonijah's party. His fellow celebrants tucked tail and ran for the hills. Then Adonijah, both humbled and scared for his life, was forced to bend the knee before his younger brother Solomon. Later, evidently not having learned his lesson, he made a fatal decision that was suspected of being treasonous. Adonijah was executed on the spot. More heads rolled as well, as Solomon, following the deathbed orders of David, removed several real or perceived threats to his throne.

Now all this politicking and bloodshed might seem highly morally suspect—and I don't disagree; it is   but often the Bible just records what happened. Good and bad. Moral and immoral. As we've noted before, the Lord works with, and often against, sinners to move his plan of salvation forward. So, with Solomon's reign now secure, and most of his known (or suspected) adversaries exiled or deep-sixed, what now? What would become of this relatively young king?

First off, Solomon made one of the best decisions of his life: he acknowledged that, on his own, he wasn't up to the task that the Lord had given him to do. In a dream, God had told Solomon, "Ask what I shall give you" (1 Kings 3:5). Now that's a wide-open invitation. He could have asked for anything. But Solomon, openly honest about his limitations, prayed for an "understanding mind" by which to govern God's people rightly (3:9). In Hebrew, an "understanding mind" is literally "a listening heart" or "hearing heart." I like to picture it as a heart with ears. For the Old Testament people, the "heart" is the core of one's being, where we think, feel, will, reason. It is the epicenter of a person. A "listening" heart means that one listens to God, heeds his word, follows where he leads. The Lord was highly pleased with this request. He told Solomon that not only would he receive a "wise and discerning mind," but God would also give him what he had *not* asked for: riches and honor.

Nor was the Lord kidding. Solomon became internationally renowned for his wisdom. Foreign dignitaries, like the Queen of Sheba, showed up on the king's doorstep to see if all the hype about him was true. It was. He took her breath away, quite literally (1 Kings 10:5). In fact, not only were the reports about the king unexaggerated, she admitted, "The half was not told me. Your wisdom and prosperity surpass the report that I heard" (1 Kings 10:7). Solomon made the kingdom so rich with gold that silver was basically worthless (10:27). He also wrote songs, composed proverbs, studied plants and animals. The man was a polymath. Summing up Solomon's fame and knowledge, the Bible says, "God gave Solomon wisdom and understanding beyond measure, and breadth of mind like the sand on the seashore, so that Solomon's wisdom surpassed the wisdom of all the people of the east and all the wisdom of Egypt" (1 Kings 4:29-30). Even allowing for hyperbole, Solomon was a king of astonishing and almost unparalleled success and erudition.

The king was also a builder. No, that's too mild. He was The Builder. There was his regal residence, a palace that took thirteen years to complete. But Solomon's magnum opus was the temple in Jerusalem. We might think of it as the tabernacle, supersized. No longer would the Lord dwell in a tent but in this permanent, ornate, holy edifice that would serve as the central sanctuary for all Israelites. Just as in the tabernacle, the temple was two-roomed, with the inner and outer sanctums (the Holy of Holies and Holy Place). Gold was everywhere. Carving of flowers and angels and various animals graced the walls and furnishings. The temple was purposefully designed to convey visually that this was paradise: the new Garden of Eden for the Adams and Eves of Israel, where they would approach God in prayer, praise, and sacrifice. Here, the Lord of heaven dwelt on earth.

This helps to explain why Jesus, talking about his body, once said, "Destroy this temple, and in three days I will raise it up" (John 2:19). Why would Jesus call his body a temple? Because, as Paul explained, "For in [Christ] the whole fullness of deity dwells bodily" (Col. 2:9). In the Old Testament, the Lord of heaven dwelt in the temple on earth, but Jesus *is* God on earth. The Son of the Father became a human being while still remaining fully divine. He is what the temple could never be: God with skin and hair, blood and bones. His temple-body was destroyed in the crucifixion but raised again in his resurrection. Therefore, the structure that Solomon built, the temple in Jerusalem, was a picture of what was to come. The Israelites approached God in the temple; God comes to us, as a man himself, in Jesus Christ.

Solomon comes across as a kind of Old Testament superman. I don't mean the cape-wearing hero, but a man of superb talent, knowledge, understanding, wealth, influence, industry, daring, and so forth. Super in every way. The most interesting man in the ancient world. Whatever over-the-top title you want to give him. We might even call him an Adam figure in that he was like a primal specimen of humanity.

On top of everything else we have mentioned, Solomon is traditionally said to have authored three of the books of the Bible: the Song of Songs (aka Song of Solomon), Ecclesiastes, and Proverbs. The first of these is a love song, full of evocative imagery, depicting the romance between the king and a woman called the Shulammite. It has long been interpreted as an allegory of the love between Christ and his bride, the church. Ecclesiastes, the most philosophical-sounding book of the Bible, ruminates on the vanity of life lived apart from fearing God and keeping his Word. And Proverbs, as the same suggests, is primarily a collection of pithy wisdom sayings that guide people into a life that conforms with the will of God. Wisdom, often personified in Proverbs, is none other than the one who is also called the Word, Glory, Messenger, and other titles in the Bible: the Son of God. Christ, as Wisdom, therefore, serves as the foundation for understanding Proverbs as a whole.

As you read through the Old Testament, you will encounter books, like Proverbs, that are called Wisdom Literature. Another book in this genre is Job, named after its main character. We do not know who wrote this book, or when, but some scholars suggest it was compiled during the reign of Solomon, which was a time when wisdom literature flourished. Job was a rich man from Uz, famous for his piety, whom Satan afflicted with a series of life-shattering losses, including the death of his children and an agonizing skin condition that left sores all over his body. Most of the book consists of speeches given alternately by Job and three of his supposed friends, all of whom try to convince Job that his suffering is deserved because of some unconfessed sin(s). The book is the most famous, penetrating reflection on suffering in all literature. Not only does it demonstrate how a godly man laments to the Lord in times of trial, but also the mysterious will of God, whose ways are beyond our ability to comprehend.

I underscore all of Solomon's success—author, builder, sage—on purpose. Why? Because of the rest of Solomon's story. The shadow side of his story. As kings tended to do in his day, Solomon had many wives. And by "many," I don't mean 5 or 10 or even 50. I mean 700, plus 300 concubines (1 Kings 11:3). The wives hailed from Egypt, Moab, Edom, and other surrounding nations. Most of these marriages were for nothing more than show, for the solidification of political alliances, as royal marriages have been throughout history. We are told, however, that Solomon "loved many foreign women" (1 Kings 11:1).

You probably don't need to be told that this became a huge problem. But let's clarify why. There are two major reasons, closely interconnected. One: long before the Israelites even had a king, the Lord had said that, when they got one, this ruler was definitely *not* supposed to "acquire many wives for himself, lest his heart turn away" (Deut. 17:17). We can all agree, I assume, that 700 qualifies as "many wives." Solomon openly thwarted what God had said. But it wasn't just the ridiculous number of marriages that was the issue. The reason for the prohibition was "lest [the king's] heart turn away." Turn away from what? From God.

That is the second, most important, reason for the prohibition against many wives. Here's what happened with Solomon.

> For when Solomon was old his wives turned away his heart after other gods, and his heart was not wholly true to the LORD his God, as was the heart of David his father. For Solomon went after Ashtoreth the goddess of the Sidonians, and after Milcom the abomination of the Ammonites. So Solomon did what was evil in the sight of the LORD and did not wholly follow the LORD, as David his father had done. Then Solomon built a high place for Chemosh the abomination of Moab, and for Molech the abomination of the Ammonites, on the mountain east of Jerusalem. And so he did for all his foreign wives, who made offerings and sacrificed to their gods (1 Kings 11:4-8).

Solomon was engaging in the age-old religious practice of what could be called "God-and-ism." He worshiped the true God *and Ashtoreth*, the true God *and Milcom*. He built the temple for the true God *and worship sites for other deities*. The technical term for this is syncretism, and sadly, it came to dominate and pollute the religious landscape of Israel for centuries.

The first commandment that the Lord gave Israel was this: "You shall have no other gods before me" (Exod. 20:3). As we have noted before, deities of the ancient world were fine with having an "open relationship" with their devotees. As long as you gave the gods or goddesses some prayer or sacrifice, you could "hook up" in worship with as many other divinities as you pleased.

Not so with Yahweh. No siree. He demanded a strict, no-exceptions, monogamous, one-God-alone fidelity. This had nothing to do with petty jealousy; it was driven by a passionate, ferocious love for humanity. He alone was, and is, God. Sure, the world is full of pseudo-deities, then as now. Some are mere phantoms of the imagination; others are devils wearing the masks of religion. Either way, all such non-gods cannot forgive, cannot answer prayers, cannot give life, cannot be God for us any more than a lie can be the truth or darkness can be light. To worship them, as did wise Solomon, is to play the fool. His love and devotion to his wives outstripped his love and devotion to the one true and living God. At the close of his life, that "hearing heart" for which he had prayed as a young man was deaf to the Word of our Lord and calcified by idolatry.

Solomon became the wisest fool.

This king's life parades before us some painful but necessary lessons. The most obvious is this: the chief threat to our well-being is the siren call of idolatry. When we fear something more than we fear God; when we love something or someone more than we do love God; when we trust something or someone more than we do God, then that person, institution, job, political party, or possession has become the object of our worship. There is room in the human heart for only one

Lord. Solomon tried to cram a whole passel of deities in his heart, as do we still today. The life of this king, then, becomes a mirror we can hold up to our own lives, to ask hard questions of ourselves. And having done so, to turn to our Lord in confession and repentance. He is always ready and willing to forgive. Indeed, he delights in doing so.

We also learn from Solomon, this seeming superman, that a human being may have multiple PhDs, billions of dollars, power, and prestige, but that person is still a sinner who often acts idiotically—and is just as much in need of forgiveness and salvation as an uneducated homeless man living alone in a squalid alley. We all stand equally in need of the mercy of God in Jesus Christ. Sin has democratized us all. Solomon needed salvation. I do. You do. All of us do.

This, then, is Solomon's story. A cautionary tale, to be sure, but also more than that. God had made a promise to David. One of his descendants would sit upon the throne and reign over an everlasting kingdom. That descendant was not Solomon, but Solomon did foreshadow him. As Solomon rode David's mule into Jerusalem as the anointed king, Jesus the Anointed rode a donkey into Jerusalem on Palm Sunday, as the crowds shouted "Hosanna to the Son of David" (Matt. 21:9). He rode in to claim his kingdom, to reign from the cross, to rise from the dead, and to take his seat at the right hand of the Father in heaven as King of kings and Lord of lords.

As we drive into the next stage of salvation history, we will meet Solomon's son and successor, a couple of big-time prophets, and a whole bunch of kings. Onward we go!

Chapter 15

Hothead Kings, Civil War, and Looming Doom

If we drove around Jerusalem shortly after Solomon's death, we'd spot a crowd of angry protestors in the street. Sick and tired of the high taxes and forced labor they had endured under Solomon, they were demanding that the next king lighten their load. Would he? We'll soon find out. We'll also find out what happens when the nation splits into north and south, international superpowers start knocking on Israel's door, and king after bad king leads God's people closer to destruction and exile.

Authors who are working up to a major plot twist will drop telltale hints along the way to alert the keen reader that something big is on the horizon. The biblical writers are no exception. Beginning already in David's reign, the narrator informs us that the unity of the dozen tribes of Israel was a fragile bond. While Solomon was king, although he tried to cement this unity, serious cracks were appearing. One of those "cracks" was an erstwhile servant of Solomon named Jeroboam; we'll get to him in a moment. Plus, there was the issue of Solomon's impressive building projects. How did he manage to get all that monumental work done? By overworking and overtaxing his people. That's how. Not exactly the way to curry his people's favor and foster unity.

So Solomon, wise but foolish, had kindled a fire of growing discontentment among his people. By the time his son Rehoboam was wearing the crown, this fire was blazing beside a huge powder keg. When the explosion came, its blast radius reached the far-flung borders of Israel and echoed for centuries afterward.

Rehoboam's first official decision set off that explosion. The discontents among his citizenry were headed by Jeroboam, whom we mentioned above. Who was he? Years before, he had been a soldier and successful leader under Solomon. But when word reached the king that a prophet had foretold that Jeroboam would one day rule over ten tribes of Israel, Solomon tried to kill him. Preferring to have his head still attached to his body, Jeroboam fled to Egypt. There he lived in exile. When Solomon was no longer a threat, Jeroboam returned home to make demands, along with his followers, that the son of Solomon lighten the yoke that his father had placed on Israel.

How did Rehoboam respond? Rejecting the wise advice of some of his elder statesmen that he should bow to the people's demands, the king instead heeded the cocky blustering of his friends. He pompously said to his people (and I'm paraphrasing), "You think things were tough under my father? By the time I'm done with you, you'll think the old days were a walk in the park." His actual words are memorable: "My father disciplined you with whips, but I will discipline you with scorpions"

(1 Kings 12:15). This arrogant and egotistical decision, like a falling sword, clove the nation in two. It also spawned an on-again-off-again civil war between north and south, and created a space where a wide variety of evils would flourish, especially idolatry.

This all began around the year 930 BC. Just to get the bird's eye view of things, here is what happened in the broader sweep of history, from 1 Kings 12 to the end of 2 Kings.

For about two more centuries, ten tribes in the northern part of the land existed independently. This nation is usually called Israel or Ephraim. We'll refer to it as the NK (Northern Kingdom). In 722 BC, the international power of the day, the Assyrians, thrashed the NK and exiled those ten tribes. If you've heard about the "lost tribes of Israel," these are the ones being referenced, though they were never really "lost." Some were exiled. The more impoverished of those tribes remained in the land. Still others migrated south, before or during the Assyrian invasion, and resettled there.

Meanwhile, in the southern part of the land, two tribes survived: Judah and Benjamin. This is the Southern Kingdom (SK), which the Bible usually calls "Judah." In 586 BC, the new superpower on the block, the Babylonians, decimated the SK and exiled those two tribes. During these approximately three and a half centuries, from 930 to 586 BC, the people of God were ruled by a handful of good kings, lots of bad kings, and a few truly horrible ones. State-sponsored worship of other gods flourished in the NK and often in the SK.

That's the big picture; let's get back to a few close-ups.

First off, on the heels of Rehoboam's fatal decision to perpetuate and expand Solomon's oppressive measures, the ten northern tribes, under the leadership of Jeroboam, said, "Fine. We'll just take our ball and go home." And homeward they went, piecing together their own country. Now this might have been fine and dandy—in fact, the Lord had said it would be (1 Kings 11)—had Jeroboam not decided that he knew better than God how and where God wanted to be worshiped.

The king was afraid that he would lose the loyalty of his subjects, not to mention his life, if they kept traveling to the SK to worship Yahweh at the temple in Jerusalem. So what did he do? He hatched the harebrained idea of erecting two golden calves at the northern and southern extremes of his kingdom, one at Dan and one at Bethel. Then he told his subjects to worship at one of those two spots instead of Jerusalem. As we discussed in Chapter 8, bulls or calves were often used as images for, or platforms for, deities in the ancient Near East. In Jeroboam's day, the deity that was all the rage was Baal, as well as his consort, Asherah. As you'll remember, when Israel tried this golden calf experiment at Mt. Sinai the first time, God just about wiped them out in anger. Now, centuries later, two more golden calves enter the picture. And the result, as you might guess, was exactly the same. When Jeroboam made these calves, he was digging his people's graves.

During a visit to Israel in February of 2022, when we stopped at the ancient city of Dan, I stood about twenty yards away from where one of these golden calves had been. Pointing to the spot, I told the group who was with me, "Right over there was not *a* sin but *The Sin* of Israel." In fact, "walking in the way of Jeroboam" became shorthand for how subsequent kings of the NK supported, promulgated, and participated in the foundational sin of idolatry.

For about two hundred years, therefore, from Jeroboam onward, Israel walked defiantly toward its demise. A total of nineteen kings reigned over the NK, some for decades, a couple for a few months, and one fellow named Zimri eked out a mini-reign of only seven days. Intrigue and tumult and bloodshed were the norm. One rather nasty queen named Jezebel, archpatroness of idolatry and hater of all things connected to Yahweh, was thrown out of a window and her body devoured in the street by a pack of wild dogs. Gruesome stuff.

The closest the NK ever came to having a king who was not heavily criticized by God was a man named Jehu. But everywhere that king went, he left a blood-bath in his wake. Interestingly, Jehu is both named and depicted in a ninth-century BC obelisk from Assyria, called the "Black Obelisk of Shalmaneser III." And what is Jehu doing? He is on his hands and knees before the Assyrian monarch. The picture says it all. The only king of the north who even came close to being faithful to the Lord ruled over a land that still had to grovel before Assyria.

The NK, in its stubborn refusal to destroy the golden calves and return in repentance to the Lord, ensured its eventual national destruction. In 722 BC, the Assyrians put the final nail in the country's coffin. Death, defeat, and deportation were the fruits of the NK's idolatry.

What about Judah, Israel's sister country in the south? How did she fare? Nineteen kings and one queen ruled over the SK. Some of these kings were carbon copies of their northern counterparts, fully enamored with worshiping the gods of other nations, polluting Jerusalem and even Yahweh's temple with idolatry. Others—thank God!—were the diametric opposite. Two stellar rulers Hezekiah and Josiah did all within their power to steer the nation onto the straight and narrow Yahweh road and keep them there. But other kings, like erratic drivers, spent half the time weaving from ditch to ditch. Although they did some good and noteworthy things during their time on the throne, they also allowed illicit worship to continue on "high places." The Bible refers frequently to these worship locations. High places were sites, scattered throughout the land, where sacrifices were made to false gods (or, more likely, to false gods *plus* Yahweh).

Over time, however, it became painfully obvious that, like their counterparts in the NK, the SK of Judah was deeply addicted to "whoring after other gods" (to use the Bible's memorable metaphor). No matter how many prophets the Lord sent to warn, rebuke, cajole, and woo his people back to fidelity and monogamy, the SK lustily hopped into the worship bed of other gods and goddesses. Finally, the Lord's longsuffering patience came to an end. Even his own house, the temple, reeked from the toxic stench of idolatry. You want to know how bad things were? Citizens of Jerusalem were sacrificing babies to a god named Molech outside Jerusalem. This was the stuff of nightmares.

It was high time for the divine axe to fall. And fall it did, over the course of several years, when God used the Babylonians to discipline his hardhearted people. This foreign superpower began taking some Judeans into exile around 600 BC, then finally sacked the city of Jerusalem, torched the temple, and led much of the population in chains in 586 BC. The last king, Zedekiah, watched as the Babylonians butchered his sons before his eyes, then they gouged out the king's eyes so that the last thing he saw was the worst thing imaginable. It was a sad end to a sad story about the ultimate sadness that always—and I mean always—comes from shoving the Lord away, time and time again, to worship the dark forces of evil that lurk behind all pseudo gods.

If you're saying to yourself, "Wow, this chapter has been a real downer!" then, yes, you are exactly right. I couldn't agree more. This is a long and dark chapter in biblical history to wade through. It's like watching someone you once loved and admired die a slow and painful death from cancer, but becoming not only weaker by the day, but meaner and grotesque in character. That's Israel in 1 and 2 Kings. We have come a long way from the time of David, back in the 900s BC, a man after God's own heart, when the nation was united, the Lord was worshiped, and the future looked bright.

Before we start sounding too glum, however, let's recollect the vital, four-word fact that always bears repeating: *God. Keeps. His. Promises.* He never says he'll do something with his fingers crossed behind his back. He never adds fine print that gives him a legal loophole to renege on what he has sworn to do. And what had the Lord, back in the days of King David, sworn to do for him, to give to him? God told David that he would not only give him a dynasty of sons and grandsons and great-grandsons to rule after him, but that eventually he would raise up a son of David, the throne of whose kingdom would endure forever. Obviously, at this point, that son had not yet graced the stage of history. Every single regal descendant of David had died in office, only to be replaced by another who likewise died in office. And, as we just noted, the last king of Judah, Zedekiah, watched in horror as his sons were slain in front of him.

If this promise of God to David was to come to fulfillment, when would it happen?

About six centuries later, that's when. One day, a Jewish girl in her teens was going about her daily routine in the tiny village of Nazareth, far up on a hillside, overlooking the lush valley of Jezreel in northern Israel. Looking up, she saw an angel standing before her, saying,

> "Greetings, O favored one, the Lord is with you!" But she was greatly troubled at the saying, and tried to discern what sort of greeting this might be. And the angel said to her, "Do not be afraid, Mary, for you have found favor with God. And behold, you will conceive in your womb and bear a son, and you shall call his name Jesus. He will be great and will be called the Son of the Most High. And the Lord God will give to him the throne of his father David, and he will reign over the house of Jacob forever, and of his kingdom there will be no end" (Luke 1:28-33).

Ah, finally! The promise, made long ago to David, and through David to all Israel, and through all Israel to the whole world, was indeed kept by God. The baby who would thenceforth be growing inside the virgin Mary's womb would be given "the throne of his father David." He would "reign over the house of Jacob forever, and of his kingdom there [would] be no end."

Jesus was the king that neither Solomon, Rehoboam, Josiah, Hezekiah, Zedekiah, nor any other descendant of David could be: the son of David *and* the Son of the Most High. God and man in one person, 100% human, 100% divine. And he reigns forever because, even when he was crucified, he could not and would not stay dead, but marched alive from his tomb three days later, leaving death behind forever. Right now, he sits on his heavenly throne, reigning from there "over the house of Jacob," that is, over the church, the community of the Messiah. God indeed keeps his promises.

To wrap this chapter up, let me remind you of something I said above, almost in passing: the Lord sent many prophets to warn, rebuke, cajole, and woo his people back to fidelity and monogamy. Before we travel any further down this historical road, we need to talk about these preachers. Who were they? What did they do? What did they say? What are their books about? Let's use the next chapter to hitch a ride with guys like Elijah, Elisha, Isaiah, Jeremiah, and others. Without their stories, the story of salvation would never have been told.

Chapter 16

The Lord's Coffee Cup
and Long Line of Preachers

The Hebrew folks in this chapter's driver's seat are a mixture of Shakespearean rhetoricians, wonderworkers, apocalyptic foretellers, and priestly preachers. Not a dull moment with them. One day they're reading the riot act to the most powerful person in the land, the next they're walking around naked as a jaybird in a sort of nonverbal sermon. Some are named, some anonymous. One left behind only twenty-one verses (Obadiah), while another bequeathed to us sixty-six chapters (Isaiah). All of them have this in common: they were God-sent preachers whose mission was to speak what the Lord had given them to say, no matter what the blessing or blowback might be.

We have been traversing some frightening landscape that's well nigh barren of hope. There was idol-crazy Jeroboam. Dog-devoured Jezebel. Blinded Zedekiah. No matter which direction we traveled, north to Israel or south to Judah, through Bethel or on the outskirts of

Jerusalem, our eyes spied high places, golden calves, or some other unholy spot where the people of God were turning their backs on Yahweh.

One has to wonder: did the Lord just wash his hands of these rebels? Did he, like a husband who's discovered his wife is having an affair, simply file for divorce and walk away to find another, more faithful, spouse? Was he angry, apathetic, disappointed, stoic? In other words, generally speaking, when the people whom God cares deeply about stray from him, how does he respond? And, to make it more personal, when *we* stray, what does our Father do?

The short answer is this: he comes after us with a ferocious, unrelenting love. He doesn't take betrayal lying down, but neither does he impulsively annihilate sinners. No, he is patient and long-suffering, heaven-bent on getting us back. God himself put it this way, "Have I any pleasure in the death of the wicked…and not rather that he should turn from his way and live?" (Ezek. 18:23). Paul writes that God "desires all people to be saved and to come to the knowledge of the truth" (1 Tim. 2:4). Aren't those some beautiful words? Whether it was with wayward Israelites or with our wayward souls still today, when we begin to stray from God or even lead hellish lives of evil, the Lord will move heaven and earth to bring us to repentance and faith in him.

How does he ordinarily do this? He sends us a preacher. Or, in the language of the Old Testament, he sends a prophet. To keep things simple, we might say that the prophets sermonized in two ways: they would foretell and forthtell. They would *foretell* in the sense of saying this or that would happen down the road.

Sometimes this was a promise of future blessing and sometimes a warning of impending doom (often both). They would also *forthtell*, that is, tell forth the will of the Lord, proclaim the truth of God. This forthtelling might be an admonition to a king, encouragement to a widow, or instruction to a person in need of healing. In addition to this oral proclamation, some prophets worked miracles or "acted out" messages, as when the prophet I mentioned above (Isaiah) walked around shoeless and unclothed to foretell visually a time of exile and deprivation.

I've always chuckled at a Hebrew expression that occurs a few times in Jeremiah's writings. In English, it reads, "From the day that your fathers came out of the land of Egypt to this day, I have persistently sent all my servants the prophets to them, day after day" (7:25). A more literal translation for "persistently" is that God was "daily rising early" and sending the prophets. I picture the Lord God, well before dawn, pouring himself a cup of celestial coffee, taking a few sips, glancing at the sunrise, then musing to himself, "Well, I guess it's about time I sent my people *another* prophet." And so he did, time and again.

As you read through 1-2 Samuel, then 1-2 Kings, you will meander through the lives of kings such as Saul, David, Solomon, Rehoboam, Jeroboam, all the way to Zedekiah. You will also hear about the ministries of several prophets. There's Samuel, Nathan, and Gad. There's Micaiah, Elijah, Elisha, and others. Along with these prophets that we know by name are some who are anonymous, often simply dubbed "a man of God." In the history we covered in the last chapter, the two

preachers who dominate the narrative are Elijah and
his successor, Elisha.

Elijah and Elisha were larger-than-life personal-
ities. They resurrected the dead, provided miraculous
amounts of food, healed the sick, called for famines
upon the land, and held showdowns with the prophets
of Baal. Elijah was such a unique person that he didn't
even exit this life in the ordinary human way. No, that
wouldn't do. Instead, he was whisked up to heaven, still
alive, in a whirlwind and chariots of fire.

His companion and protégé, Elisha, carried on
Elijah's work. He didn't leave this world with the fanfare
of his predecessor—like everyone else, Elisha died—but
so powerful were his prophetic gifts that he resurrected
a person posthumously. Yes, you read that right. During
an enemy attack, when a man was being hurriedly buried, his body was dropped into Elisha's grave. When the
dead man's body touched the prophet's bones, the man
sprung back to life. Even while dead, Elisha gave life.

When you read the Gospels, if you bear in mind
the stories of these two prophets, you will notice par-
allels between Elijah and John the Baptist as well as
between Elisha and Jesus. For instance, John comes "in
the spirit and power of Elijah" (Luke 1:17). He even
copycatted Elijah in his hairy coat and leather belt
(2 Kings 1:8; Matt. 3:4). In the Old Testament, Elijah
passed on his mantle to Elisha near the Jordan River. In
the Gospels, when John baptized Jesus in the Jordan, the
former's role began to diminish so the spotlight could
be solely on Jesus. And, like the healing, feeding, and
resurrecting miracles of Elisha, Jesus performed similar but even greater miracles. Indeed, so prophet-like
was the ministry of Jesus that many people mistakenly

thought he was one of the prophets of old, come back to life (Matt. 16:14). We see, therefore, how the Lord was crafting the salvation story of Elijah and Elisha so that it provided a blueprint that would be followed and greatly expanded by John and Jesus.

Of course, Elijah and Elisha were only two of many prophets that the Lord sent to encourage the faithful and to call the unfaithful back to himself. The other prophets are sometimes called "Writing Prophets" because their written words, or collections of their writings, have come down to us in the books of the Old Testament that are named after them. Typically, we divide them into two groups: major and minor prophets. The division has nothing to do with their relative importance, only with the extent of their writings. So, a major prophet = a bigger book, and a minor prophet = a smaller book. The minor prophets are also sometimes called "the Book of the Twelve" because the Hebrew writings of the dozen minor prophets all fit onto a single scroll ("book").

These minor prophets, who were they? Their names are Hosea, Joel, Amos, Obadiah, Jonah, Micah, Nahum, Habakkuk, Zephaniah, Haggai, Zechariah, and Malachi. A few of them were contemporaries, but together, the ministries of these dozen men stretched for centuries. If Joel is dated to the 800s BC, as some suggest, he would be the earliest of them. And the latest is Malachi, who wrote around 430 BC. Keep in mind, too, that it's not as if these fellows scribbled "Tuesday, March 5, 750 BC" or some other date onto their scrolls. Dating is often just an educated guess based on hints in their writings as to historical circumstances.

Who was their audience? Some of the twelve preached to God's people in the north, some preached to Judah in the south, and several of them addressed oracles to nearby or distant nations, like the Assyrians or Edomites. Of the twelve minor prophets, Jonah is unique because his book is mainly the narrative about this prophet's mulish refusal to preach to the Assyrians, his adventure at sea, three days in a fish's belly, and subsequent pity party when God refused to destroy the very people to whom Jonah had finally preached! Jonah reads like a dark comedy. And the end? It's a biblical cliffhanger.

The major prophets are really the trio of Isaiah, Jeremiah, and Ezekiel. Two more are often thrown into this grouping: Daniel and Lamentations. The latter of these, Lamentations, is not a prophet at all, but a lengthy, heart-wrenching lament psalm penned after Jerusalem was bulldozed by the Babylonians and her people massacred or hauled into exile. Daniel, while a prophet, is a different variety of prophetic book; we will talk more about him and his book in a future chapter.

Regarding Isaiah, it would not be much of an exaggeration to say that his book is the Old Testament prophetic canvas upon which the colors of the New Testament are painted. By one estimate, all but three of the sixty-six chapters of Isaiah are quoted, alluded to, or echoed in the NT. Isaiah's writings loom so large in New Testament books because of how this prophet foretells, in poetically striking ways, the dawn of the kingdom of God that comes when the Savior is born. Writing in the 700s BC, Isaiah speaks of the virgin birth of the Messiah, that he is the Servant of the Lord, the promised Son of David, the bringer of new creation, and the innocent victim who is put to death for the sins of humanity (see especially Isaiah 53). If we lost all other biblical books, but retained Isaiah, we would still have enough material to teach and preach for a life-time about the Son of God and his work for us. Isaiah prophesied to his own generation, but he wrote in such a way that, whenever his readers might live, they sense that he is directly addressing them. In addition, Isaiah is rightly ranked among some of the loftiest, most beau-tiful poetry ever composed in any language.

When we read Jeremiah, we come away with con-flicted emotions. Because he tells us so much about his life and the pains he endured—persecution, exile, imprisonment, forbidden to marry or have children—we feel like we really know the man. And he wrote *a lot*; by word count, his book is the longest in the Bible. Because in his lifetime his preaching was largely ignored, his ministry can seem thankless. He warned that the Babylonians would destroy Jerusalem, then lived through that harrowing ordeal. One can't help but pity him. But God also used Jeremiah to deliver some powerful good news. He foretold the coming Son of David, the Messiah, who would restore the scattered people of God. He also spoke of the new covenant, which Jesus inaugurated—the covenant that cannot be broken because God himself upholds it. Like many of the people whom our Father has used throughout his-tory, Jeremiah probably never realized in his lifetime how much joy and hope his words would bring future generations. As a kind of tip of the hat to this forlorn prophet, the New Testament honors Jeremiah by award-ing him the longest quotation of any Old Testament book by a New Testament writer, as Hebrews 8:8-12 quotes Jeremiah 31:31-34 regarding the new covenant.

If you're new to the Bible, this may come as a surprise, but on occasion the prophets employ sexually graphic metaphors to condemn Israel's spiritual infidelity. The third figure among the major prophets, Ezekiel, is the unrivaled master of this racy rhetoric, as you can tell by reading chapters 16 and 23 of his book. (Don't say I didn't warn you.) This prophet also loves to use the Hebrew word *gillulim* as a nickname for false gods; we might render it "dung-deities" or "crap-gods."

Obviously, Ezekiel was a preacher who knew how to deliver memorable sermons. His people needed that. Ezekiel was a contemporary of Jeremiah; both lived through the Babylonian destruction of Jerusalem in 586 BC. Ezekiel, however, experienced this from afar, for he had been swept up in an early wave of exiles and hauled off to Babylon. His 48-chapter work is bookended by visions of the temple, one bad, one good. Early on, he sees the Lord vacating his temple in Jerusalem since it had been polluted by idolatry. In the closing section of Ezekiel's book, however, the Lord returns to a new, ideal temple that is a symbol of the Messiah's kingdom and church.

Elijah. Elisha. Isaiah. Jeremiah. Ezekiel. Hosea and the other eleven minor prophets. If only for a few seconds, we have welcomed each of them into the driver's seat. But I have a confession to make: in rereading this chapter, I'm disappointed. Not by the content. I don't mean that. I mean that this tiny, fleeting introduction to the prophets seems grossly inadequate, given their huge importance in the salvation story.

Think of it this way. Suppose you had a handful of guests over for dinner. Adjacent to where you are sitting with your company is the dining room. On the table in that room are several bottles of vintage wine. Plates are heaped with the finest meats and vegetables and fruits you can imagine. A mouthwatering dessert has been prepared. And all you can do, at this point, is provide your guests with a sample spoonful to whet their appetite. Just a taste. To get more, they'll need to get up and move to the other room for the feast that awaits them.

This chapter has been that spoonful, that taste. Move next door, therefore, into the dining room of the prophets. Eat their words. Drink in their wisdom. Make a meal of their sermons. It's the finest feast you'll find.

So dig in. You can thank me later.

Chapter 17

Bye-Bye Babylon and Hello to Rebuilding Jerusalem

Hop in. We've got some serious miles to cover. North and east to Babylon we'll go, following the Israelite version of the Trail of Tears. Daniel, the lion tamer and apocalyptic man, will give us a glimpse into Babylon. Then we'll drive back toward the desolate rubble of Jerusalem to see a struggling small community of Jews attempt to piece life back together, rebuild the temple, and carve out a little niche of hope for better days to come.

Two chapters ago, we left things in a bit of a mess. Okay, actually, a *huge* mess. After Israel's centuries-long drift toward destruction, God finally decided to deliver to his people a painful wake-up call. It came in the form of the superpower Babylon, headed by King Nebuchadnezzar, wielding a sledgehammer against Jerusalem and the temple. Bang, bang, bang. When all was done, the city and sanctuary were heaps of rubble. The walls flattened. Most of the people were deported. And thus began the woeful, seventy-year Babylonian exile.

In this chapter, we want to talk about how and why the Israelites were given the opportunity, after seven decades, to retrace their steps to Jerusalem. But before we do that, we need to talk briefly about one of the most interesting men in the Bible. He goes by two names: one given him by his Babylonian overlords (Belteshazzar) and the other by his Hebrew parents (Daniel). We know him better by that latter name.

Like his contemporary Ezekiel—remember him from the last chapter?—Daniel was among the early wave of exiles to Babylon. He arrived in that foreign city around the end of the sixth century BC (597-ish). Daniel was quite the guy: pious man of prayer, erudite sage, counselor of kings, dream interpreter, apocalyptic prophet, and, most famously, companion of lions. The book that bears his name is divided into two main sections: Chapters 1-6 record narratives involving Daniel's life and misadventures in Babylon, while Chapters 7-12 record multiple visions revolving around the rise and fall of kingdoms.

Are you up for some gripping stories? Then grab the nearest Bible or tap on your YouVersion Bible app and scroll to Daniel 1-6. Here, you'll read all about Daniel and his three Jewish compatriots: Shadrach, Meshach, and Abednego. These four remained faithful to God while far from home, even in the most trying, and potentially fatal, of circumstances. For instance, Daniel's friends, when tossed into a massive blazing furnace for refusing to bow before an idolatrous statue, were preserved by God. In fact, not even a stitch of their clothing burned. Daniel himself, when he broke the king's law by praying to the true God, was jailed for a night in a den full of hungry lions. As happened to his three friends, Daniel too was kept safe by the Lord; God made these beasts as harmless as purring kittens. Alongside these stories of fidelity and danger, we learn that Daniel had the gift of interpreting dreams—a gift he exercised for the king of Babylon in Daniel 2.

In the remainder of Daniel's book, Chapters 7-12, things get strange. There are visions of beasts, heavenly court scenes, looming catastrophes, and the rising kingdom of the Messiah, who is described as one like a "Son of Man." These visions are, to modern readers, some wild and bizarre stuff. They belong to the genre of literature called "apocalyptic." Other parts of the Old Testament, like sections of Ezekiel and Zechariah and Isaiah, are in this genre as well. So is the last book of the Bible, Revelation, which is sometimes called "The *Apocalypse* of St. John."

The word "apocalyptic" is derived from a Greek word meaning "disclosure, unveiling, revelation." To new students of the Bible's apocalyptic literature—and often to experienced ones, as well—it can feel like you're reading a literary cocktail of science fiction, *Lord of the Rings*, and *Animal Farm*, seasoned with plenty of angels and demons. The basic purposes of these kinds of writings are to tell us (1) what is *really* going on now beneath the outward veil of history and (2) what will happen in the future. It does this, however, not in a straightforward way but with highly symbolic, colorful, and often frightening language.

In the second half of his book, this is what Daniel does. He foretells the coming of several successive world kingdoms, the rulers of these kingdoms, the persecution of God's people, and the establishment of the worldwide kingdom of the "Son of Man" in Daniel 7. This title,

Son of Man, is used by Jesus in the Gospels to refer to himself. The "Ancient of Days" in Daniel's vision is our Father in heaven, who gives to Jesus, the "Son of Man," the kingdom over which he reigns. Daniel's writings made a huge and lasting impact on subsequent parts of the Bible, especially Revelation, where Daniel is quoted or alluded to multiple times. In fact, when you read Revelation, it can seem like you're studying an updated and expanded version of Daniel, with some extra material mixed in.

There is much more that we could say about Daniel, his experiences and wisdom and visions, but perhaps this has whet your appetite to learn more. For now, we need to ride through the rest of the salvation story. Some questions arise. If the Israelites were in Babylon for about seventy years, how were they freed? Did all of them return home? And those who went back to Jerusalem, what did they find when they returned? What challenges and setbacks did they face? And who were their leaders and prophets?

First off, there was a major political change. The Israelites had been living alongside their Babylonian captors for decades, but now these erstwhile overlords became underlings. In 539 BC, a new world power took charge: the Persians. Led by Cyrus, they swept through and became the apex people in the region. History was unfolding just as the Lord had promised it would (see Isaiah 44:28-45:1). Neither the Babylonian losers nor Persian winners were aware of this, of course. No doubt the Persians were flexing their muscles, proud of their new alpha status. Little did they know that, flex as they might, they were mere instruments in the hands of the

Lord of history, who raises and lowers kingdoms as he sees fit. Babylon down, Persia up.

Persian rule was, overall, a breath of fresh air for the Jews. (By the way, around this time, the Israelites came to be called Jews, a name derived from the region called Yehud, around Jerusalem.) But don't get the idea that the Jews were suddenly a free people under the Persians. No, but they did have greater liberty under this new regime.

The prime example of this greater liberty was the "Decree [or Edict] of Cyrus," issued in 538 BC. The Persian king allowed the Jews, should they choose, to leave Babylon and resettle in Jerusalem. You might assume that this decree was welcomed with parades and fireworks by the exiled Jews. "Hooray! After seventy years of waiting, we can finally go home!" But think about it; suppose you were in a similar situation. Let's say your Jewish Grandma and Grandpa talked nostalgically about the "good old days" back in Jerusalem, but you? Your parents? The younger generation had been born and raised in Babylon. You were comfortably at home in its culture, streets, commerce, language. You had non-Jewish friends and neighbors, maybe even a wife or husband from there. Babylonian life was the only life you had ever known. The opportunity to return "home" might sound appealing, theoretically, but your *home* was, and always had been, Babylon.

With that in mind, it comes as no surprise that while some Jews took advantage of the opportunity to migrate back to Jerusalem, most said, "Thanks, but no thanks. We're comfortable here." Indeed, Babylon would be home to a significant portion of the Jewish people, as well as the center of later Jewish scholarship, for centuries to come. There were groups of Jews, however, who welcomed the Decree of Cyrus. They packed up their belongings and left Babylon behind, making the long and arduous journey to their homeland, which had now become a Persian province.

These Jewish "pilgrims," as we might call them, arrived to find Jerusalem looking like a bombed-out ghost town with only a few scattered folks living nearby. The city walls were broken down. The temple and its altar a heap of ruins. And some of the neighboring nations weren't particularly happy that the Jews had returned. All in all, it was not much of a hopeful homecoming. But, rolling up their sleeves, the people of God went to work. The first order of business was rebuilding the altar. Much later, after a years-long delay and some prophetic arm-twisting from Haggai and others, the entire temple was completed and dedicated. This temple, in expanded form, would last about another six hundred years, until the Romans razed it in AD 70. Afterward, the walls of Jerusalem were rebuilt so the city, though still far from impregnable, had a measure of defense. It was a good restart for life in Jerusalem.

In English Bibles, after the books of Ezra and Nehemiah, you will find a short book entitled Esther. Set in Persia in the 400s BC, this is the story of a wise and brave Jewish woman named Esther, who became queen to King Ahasuerus, traditionally identified as Xerxes I. As the story unfolds, we learn that a plot is hatched by a Persian official named Haman, an enemy of the Jews, to eradicate

God's people. Counseled and encouraged by her relative Mordecai, Queen Esther risks her life to save the lives of her people, with grand success. The story is a literary masterpiece, complete with intrigue, reversals, and the bad guy getting his just desserts. Esther provides the historical background of the annual Jewish festival of Purim.

Most of the history of these Jewish pilgrims is recorded in two Old Testament books Ezra and Nehemiah, named after their respective authors. Though both of these men were leaders, and their work overlapped, God used them in different ways to shepherd his little flock of believers.

Ezra was a priest and scribe. We might picture him as a Bible scholar and man of the temple. He taught the Torah, admonished his fellow Jews when they were going astray, and interceded for them in prayer. Unlike Ezra, Nehemiah was neither a priest nor scribe. He had once been a personal servant of the king, his cupbearer. When he received depressing reports about the state of Jerusalem, he asked permission to travel there and remedy the situation. The king said yes, and off Nehemiah went. The erstwhile cupbearer was now a construction overseer. More than that, he was appointed governor of this little Jewish province. As such, among other tasks, Nehemiah directed the reconstruction of the defenses around Jerusalem. The wall, down and decrepit for so long, was soon raised up and fortified.

As you read about Ezra and Nehemiah's labors in Jerusalem, it becomes painfully obvious that life in this rebuilt and fledgling city was anything but easy. Nearby neighbors were playing dirty politics by writing slanderous letters back to Persia to undermine the construction work of the Jews. Some of the Jews themselves, leaders and otherwise, weren't exactly shining models of fidelity. For example, intermarriage with non-Jews was a major issue facing the community. There were problems at the temple as well. A later prophet in Jerusalem, Malachi, complained about lazy priests who treated the altar and its offerings irreverently. Nehemiah also laments that certain prophets and a prophetess named Noadiah used intimidation tactics to stymie his work. Judging by what we can tell of Nehemiah's brash personality, however, good luck with making him back down!

All of these challenges, in combination with the day-to-day struggles of any small and isolated community, must have made many of these returnees wonder things like, "We are barely eking out a living in and around Jerusalem, so was it really worth the sacrifice to leave Babylon and resettle here? When will this great and awesome day of the Lord, promised by the prophets, come to pass? We have no king now, no descendant of David on the throne—no throne at all!—so how will the Lord fulfill his promise to raise up the Son of David, the Messiah?" These are all understandable questions. These Jewish believers had suffered much and waited long.

How much longer, O Lord, would they have to wait?
A few decades?
A century?
Several centuries?

We know the answer to that question—and we know it with precision. As we hop out of the car and wave goodbye to Ezra and Nehemiah, we will turn our attention in the next chapter to The End that is really and truly The Beginning. It looks like our journey is nearly over.

Chapter 18

Greeks, Romans, and Jewish Hammer Time

Throughout our trip together, we've been hitchhiking with patriarchs, sages, prophets, and priests, but in this last chapter, we'll be riding alongside different kinds of people: Alexander the Great, Antiochus IV Epiphanes, and Judas Maccabeus. You've heard of the first of these, no doubt, but the other two might be strangers to you. No worries. We'll make brief introductions in this chapter. In the big scheme of things, our time is short. The ride through the salvation story is mere miles from its conclusion. So let's barrel through the last few curves and prepare to park this car in Bethlehem, where our journey will finally end.

Grab the nearest Bible and find where the Old Testament ends and the New Testament begins. You'll see there's not much there. A handful of pages. Maybe a few charts or maps. With a flick of your index finger, you can move from Malachi 4 to Matthew 1 in a couple of seconds. You should know, however, that those "couple of seconds" are really about 400+ years.

Welcome to what is often called the "Intertestamental Period," that is, the time "inter" (=between) the Old and New Testaments. It's a fascinating epoch of history. Though the historical twists and turns are not recorded in the Bible itself, we know from other writings what went down during those four centuries. So that we can better understand the finale of our story, and how God was setting the stage for the birth and ministry of Jesus the Messiah, let's get a feel for the major movers and shakers of this period. We'll also take a peek at some popular Jewish literature of this time.

First, what do we *not* know? We don't know much about what happened among the Jews for the first hundred years of this period, from around 430 to 330 BC. Based on what we can piece together, the small community of Jews, centered around Jerusalem, lived in relative peace. They farmed and raised flocks and herds; engaged in trade and commerce; remained on good terms with their Persian overlords; and kept on waiting for God to make good on his promises to send the Messiah. So, for about a century, time ticked on. Not much happened.

Then, Alexander happened. That is, Alexander the Great. This young Macedonian king, with his fighting forces, began steamrolling through region after region as undefeated conquerors. By the time of his death in 323 BC, at the age of thirty-three years, Alexander held sway over a vast empire, encompassing Asia Minor, Mesopotamia, and Egypt. Basically, the entire Persian empire, plus some. While Alexander's exploits rightly earned him the title "the Great," what mainly concerns us is what his victory over Persia meant for the Jews. They were beholden to a new regime; that was obvious.

Much more serious, however, was that God's chosen people faced a new challenge—a challenge far more formidable and life-altering than "Who's the new superpower in charge?"

I'm speaking of the challenge called Hellenization, that is, the "Greekifying" of peoples and regions, including the Jews. And, let me tell you, Hellenization took the world by the horns.

Years ago, while en route to Novosibirsk, Siberia, where I would serve as a visiting lecturer for a few weeks, I stopped in Moscow for a long layover. A local missionary gave me a tour of the city. Everywhere we went, I began to notice telltale signs of a modern equivalent to ancient Hellenization—namely, Americanization. We walked past fast-food joints like McDonald's and New York Pizza. We heard American pop songs piped through store speakers. Russians were wearing American-brand clothing. Later, while watching movies with my students in Siberia during the evening, I noticed all the movies were from Hollywood, just dubbed over in Russian. Of course, such Americanization is not restricted to Russia. Recently, on a trip to Israel, our tour guide took us to an Elvis Presley-themed café on the outskirts of Jerusalem. Worldwide, American literature, entertainment, and language filter into other cultures, leaving them, in ways great and small, changed.

That is what happened, in the years after Alexander's conquests, with Hellenization. For instance, the Greek language spread everywhere. Not many generations after Alexander, Jews in Egypt began to translate the Hebrew Bible into Greek—first the Torah, then gradually the other books. This first-ever Bible translation, known as the Septuagint, ended up being used all over the ancient world by those Jews for whom Greek was their mother tongue. In fact, when New Testament authors quote or allude to the Old Testament, the influence of the Septuagint is unmistakable. But Hellenization was not restricted to the Greek language. Hellenistic ideas about entertainment, athletics, the human body, religion, politics, literature—you name it—became the cultural waters in which peoples swam, including the Jews.

While these Greek influences were hoorayed by some Jews, they were booed by others. Tensions began to mount between the pro-Greek and anti-Greek parties. And these tensions finally came to a head a little over a century and a half after Alexander. The Jews had, for some time, been under the control of the descendants of one of Alexander's generals. These Seleucids, as they were called, lived north of Jerusalem in Syria. One of their leaders, Antiochus IV Epiphanes, sparked the proverbial fire that led to a fiery revolt in 167 BC. Basically, Antiochus acted like a tyrant. He tried to un-Jew the Jews, to thoroughly "Greekify" them, by prohibiting circumcision, Sabbath observance, and other biblical laws. He also defiled the Jerusalem temple by offering a pig on the altar and had his soldiers visit Jewish villages to force them to make sacrifices to Hellenistic deities. This, finally, brought the hammer down on Antiochus.

That "hammer" was a priestly family of Jews, first led by the patriarch, Mattathias, and then by his son, Judas. This family was nicknamed the Maccabees, which means "hammer" in Hebrew. And hammer they did. For several years, through guerilla warfare and brave frontal assaults, the Maccabees led other Jewish soldiers in a victorious revolt against their Syrian oppressors. It was, in truth, just as much an assault against outsiders (Syrians) as against insiders (pro-Hellenistic Jews). In time, the temple was retaken, cleansed, and rededicated; Jews today still celebrate this event every December at Hannukah, which means "dedication." After years of fighting, the Syrians and Jews came to a peace agreement. Then, for almost a century, God's people enjoyed an independence they had not experienced in well over four hundred years (586-165 BC). If you'd like to read a blow-by-blow account of this period of Jewish history, you'll find it in two different versions: 1 Maccabees and 2 Maccabees, both written in this Intertestamental Period. These books are among the popular Jewish literature of this era, which we will talk more about in just a moment.

First, let's wrap up our history. As has happened to many revolutionary movements in history, what begins well does not always end well. The century or so of Jewish independence began as a righteous uprising against those who defiled God's temple and abrogated his laws, but over time, it devolved into childish and selfish infighting among those Jews in power. Egos got in the way. Power politics led to bloodshed, even to the crucifixion of fellow Jews. By 63 BC, when Rome, the next superpower, showed up at Jerusalem, they had no problem ending the century of Jewish independence.

Let's suppose you are a first-century Jew, living in or around Jerusalem, with a knowledge of your nation's history. You know, for instance, that your people, for about half a millennium, have been under a whole sequence of foreign powers: Babylonians, Persians, Greeks, Syrians, and now the Romans. Are you free? No. Are you independent? No. Basically, you're living "in exile" on your native soil. Yet you know from the Torah, the Prophets, the Psalms, and the books of Samuel and Kings, that the Lord God of Israel had promised to send a descendant of David to reign over the kingdom of God. You know this promise goes all the way back to the Seed that the Lord swore to send for Adam and Eve. The expectation for this Seed's arrival has been mounting. There's even been whisperings of his birth in David's hometown, about three decades before. What's more, down at the Jordan River, east of Jerusalem, a strange prophet has shown up, the first prophet in centuries. His name is John. He has been baptizing and calling people to repent, to prepare for the arrival of the Messiah. And now, on top of all this, word on the street has it that a traveling rabbi from Galilee, Jesus of Nazareth, has been teaching with authority and working miracles—even giving sight to the blind! Could he be the long-promised, long-awaited Son of God, come to redeem his people and inaugurate the divine kingdom?

Were you a first-century Jew, with a knowledge of the Bible, some history under your belt, and a fair grasp of current goings-on, those might well have been your thoughts. And good thoughts they would have been. Right on target, in fact. We will come back to them in our closing pages.

To finish up this chapter, let's suppose we could take a drive over to a first-century Barnes and Noble scroll-store in Jerusalem, sip on a cup of Zion's best coffee, and browse through the shelves. What would we see? What were people reading back then? And how did these scrolls influence the general Jewish populace?

We would see, for instance, a few copies of 1 and 2 Maccabees, which we mentioned above. These make for some gripping historical reading, full of breathtaking battle scenes and gory martyrdoms. On another shelf, labeled "Wisdom Literature," we could unroll the scroll of the Wisdom of Solomon or the Wisdom of Jesus ben Sirach (not to be confused with Jesus of Nazareth). Here we could mull over line upon line of proverbial-type sayings that contain deep insights into God and human nature. All three of these writings, along with many others, are included in what is called The Apocrypha.

When we're done there, we might mosey on over to some scrolls that could be called "Old Testament Expansions." The titles on this shelf retell certain sections from the Old Testament. They often tack on traditions or narratives not included in the original. Jubilees, for example, retells much of the history that is recorded in Genesis and Exodus, but with certain parts abbreviated and others expanded. On these same shelves would be select portions of the Greek translation of the Old Testament, the Septuagint, which has extra sections in Daniel and Esther.

When you wander around this Jerusalem scrollstore some more, you'll see there is a wide range of Jewish popular literature. There are many scrolls in the genre called "Testaments," such as the Testament of the Twelve Patriarchs. In another section, you'll find scroll upon scroll of apocalyptic literature (remember, we talked about that type of writing when discussing Daniel?). Prominent among these is 1 Enoch, a book that was known by the early Christians, and even quoted by Jude, a New Testament author. Are you into philosophy? Especially philosophy with a biblical accent? Step right up. On another shelf are the many works of Philo, a Jewish philosopher who lived in Egypt about the same time as Jesus was living and teaching in Judea. We could spend all afternoon in this Jerusalem scroll-store, perusing manuscripts of psalms and hymns, adventures and theology, apocalypses and Bible-like storytelling.

What do all these manuscripts reveal to us? The thoughts, beliefs, fears, hopes, traditions, songs, and practices of the people among whom Jesus was born. That's what. Even the way they translated the Bible into Greek is a window into the Jewish mind. Therefore, just as getting to know the Old Testament story of salvation is absolutely necessary to understanding its fulfillment in Jesus, so also getting to know the history immediately before Jesus was born and the popular literature of his day is helpful for grasping the impact that he made on his contemporaries and how they heard his message.

That last sentence is why this chapter is important. During the 400 years leading up to the birth of Jesus, our Father was preparing his people for the Savior's arrival. He set the world stage. He orchestrated events. He made sure everything was in place. He even made sure the Old Testament was translated into Greek. That way, when the New Testament was written in Greek, the authors could easily quote from a version many, if not most, of their hearers were already familiar with.

Now, here we are. Eighteen chapters into this story. Take a breath. Get ready. Stick out your thumb. We have one final, short ride to hitch. And the driver approaching—well, it turns out he's the one we've been waiting for, all along.

Afterword

Down rolls the window as the dust from the
approaching tires settles around us. Engine's
purring. The sun is high in that Judean sky.
Bend down and peer in. There he is, in the
driver's seat: the Man. "Hop in," he says, in
a voice that seems both strange and famil-
iar. So in we hop, not knowing whether to
look straight ahead or stare in awe at his
face. We steal a glance at his hands on the
steering wheel, sleeves ever so slightly riding
up his arms. Yes, there they are: a scar on
his right wrist, a scar on his left. No missing
those wounds. We know with whom we ride.
The car eases forward, dancing through the
gears, as the landscape unfolds before us.
"So," he begins, "I hear you've been waiting
for me...."

Indeed, we have. And here we are, at the end, knowing
that this is really just the beginning. He had been a long
time in coming, this Seed of Eve, Seed of Abraham, Seed
of David, who showed up in our dark and forlorn world
as the Seed of Mary. But God never is in a hurry. Like
Aslan in the Chronicles of Narnia, Jesus "calls all times

soon." Tomorrow? Soon. Ten thousand years hence? Soon. It's all soon to the one who is the same yesterday, today, and forever.

In the *yesterday* of Genesis through Malachi, he was the same. The Son of God, along with the Father and Holy Spirit, made a promise that he would keep. In ways large and small, by signs and wonders and prophesies, he was getting everything in place. Choosing a people. Establishing a line of kings. Calling prophets. Having psalms composed. By the time the Son of God was ready also to become the Son of Mary, the people of Israel knew more than enough to recognize him. The basic black-and-white pattern of who he would be and what he would do was clearly sketched on the pages of the Old Testament. All that remained was for him to appear in full color.

So he did, in the *today* of the New Testament. No longer the promise-maker, he was now also the promise-keeper. Indeed, he was the promise of God *in the flesh*. Heaven married earth in Jesus, God becoming man while still remaining God. You have hitched many a ride through the Old Testament; now I hope you do the same with the New Testament. Ride along with Matthew, Mark, Luke, and John as they each tell you, in their distinctive ways, about our Lord. Sit with Paul the Apostle as he unpacks the full implications of Jesus and his salvation for us. Enjoy a few brief miles with Peter and James and Jude. Then, when you're ready for a truly strange and beautiful ride, get in the car with John as he drives you through the kaleidoscopic terrain of Revelation.

In the *yesterday* of the Old Testament and the *today* of the New Testament, you will meet the Lord

Jesus Christ, who *forever* passionately, furiously, and devotedly loves you. Imagine that! The God of all creation, who has existed for all time—indeed, before time—knows you and calls you and loves you. There is no miracle more astounding than that. He planned, from all eternity, to create you. He also made sure that he paid for every wrong you have ever done, as well as for every good that you left undone, by his death on the cross. But dying was not the end. On the third day, he walked out of the tomb, fully alive again, with a physically glorious body, to show that death did not win. Death lost. Sin lost. Satan lost. Jesus is triumphant. And he is triumphant for you.

So hop in with Jesus. Let's roll. He is the one who will truly get us home.

General Index

Scripture Index

More Best Sellers from Chad Bird.

—

Find these titles
and more at 1517.org/**shop**

Listen to Chad Bird on the 1517 Podcast Network.

www.1517.org/**podcasts**